Learning to Pray From the Psalmist

Arthur E. Parry, Ph.D.

PublishAmerica
Baltimore

First printing

ISBN: 1-4137-4402-8
PUBLISHED BY PUBLISHAMERICA, LLLP
www.publishamerica.com
Baltimore

Printed in the United States of America

For

My wife of nearly fifty years, Patricia, whose love, sharing in the Christian walk, and being a help-mate through life, is gratefully acknowledged.

FOREWORD

Learning to Pray from the Psalmist, by Arthur E. Parry, Ph.D., sings out to the reader with the joy of confessional prayer. In this unusual, unique approach to the Psalms, Dr. Parry approaches each Psalm with a hermeneutical method, allowing the reader to develop not only a coherent, comprehensive understanding of the truth assertions of the Psalms, but also a confessional, consistent relationship with the Lord. Ultimately, the reader learns to pray along with the Psalmist, establishing a discourse conversation with God. Parry's method first reveals the unveiling of *truth* in the Psalms. He does not ask Pilate's question, "What is truth?" Having been associated with Dr. Parry as a colleague at LeTourneau University, and having presented and published papers with him, on "Meat-Ethical Questions" and "Codes of Ethics," I know he personally deepened his relationship with Christ, as he wrote this book, because he answers the ultimate meta-ethical question by living it: "Who do you say I am? –You are the Christ!" Secondly, his method develops an insight into the transformational *effect* of the Psalmist's spiritual life, a deepening awareness of the valleys and mountains, the joy and stormy seas, the reader will also experience in this journey, as the reader identifies with the Psalmist, whether the *response* is favorable or unfavorable. Finally, the result of analyzing the Psalm will be a *prayer,* strengthening the relationship of the reader to the Lord, and applying the wisdom of the Psalms into the reader's daily life. This book will guide the reader step by step through the Psalms with a devotional, journal response to each question at the end of each section. For the reader's guidance and reflection, the book contains two indexes. The first will be in the order of the chapters and Psalms within each chapter; and the second will list the Psalms numerically for easy reference. The reader should experience an abundance of grace and joy, when one's heart, mind, and soul are broken, for this is nothing less than the hope of our Lord, Jesus Christ.

Harvey E. Solganick, Ph.D.
Professor of Philosophy and Literature
Master Faculty, Graduate and Professional Studies
School of Arts and Sciences
LeTourneau University
Longview, Texas
May 11, 2004

Table of Contents

Chapter 1
How Do We Learn to Pray?

As believers in the Lord Jesus we want to obey Him and follow what is stated in God's Word. However, we want to be able to talk with God as the Psalmists did. They told Him their problems, their fears, and their hopes. They asked for His leading and strength in all situations. When they committed a problem to Him, they were able to rest in His promises and His faithfulness and leave it with Him.

We want to be able to be so closely connected with our Heavenly Father that we, too, can converse with Him as they did. The Psalmists are real people in all kinds of situations having dialogue with God and responding in faith and hope.

We will, therefore, examine each of the Psalms to learn how God spoke to the Psalmist and how he responded. From these experiences of the Psalmist we will pray, ourselves, as He leads, and directs us.

The reader is encouraged to read each Psalm first, before looking at the book observations. He or she should try to understand the Psalm, why it was written, to whom, what were the circumstances, what was the mental and spiritual condition of the Psalmist at the beginning and, then, at the conclusion of the Psalm. How did he change? How did he experience God's answers and His promises. Is what God did for the Psalmist possible for us? If not, why not? If yes, why isn't it happening?

By doing this, we are learning to pray from the Psalmist.

Chapter 2
God and the Reader/Believer

Eleven Psalms have to do with the subject of God and the Psalmist and apply to us as believers. The Psalms in this group are 20, 21, 42, 55, 23, 37, 43, 44, 62, 63, and 75.

In each of these we want to identify the following:

1. What is the *truth* of the Psalm?
2. What are the *issues and points* in the Psalm?
3. What is the *effect on the Psalmist*?
4. *How am I like or unlike the Psalmist*?
5. What is *my response* to what he has understood and written?
6. What is *my prayer* as a result?

(Each Psalm will be analyzed in the same manner).

Psalm 20

Truth- In all but two lines, God is the subject of the sentence or one clause in the sentence. In the other two lines, one is about what *foolish* men trust in, and the statement that even those will be made to fail, by the Lord. In other words, it is all about God.

Issues and points — God hears, He helps, He lifts up and supports the Psalmist.

Effect on the Psalmist — He knows God hears and He will help when he prays.

How am I like/unlike the Psalmist? I am a man as he was, but I have the privilege of knowing my risen Lord and he lived only by faith in God without this additional reality. But, do I have the complete faith in my God as he does?

My response — As a reader/believer I must recognize the imperative of centering my thoughts and my heart entirely on the Lord.

My prayer:
Lord, what I need, what I want to do,
Has never been as important as You.
For Your grace, Your power, Your Love,
Conquer the petty claims I have.
Oh, draw me close, Oh, Lord, I pray,
Remove the selfish desires from me,
Cause me to look up to Your holiness,
Prevent me from thinking only of my own.
Please accept my humble prayer
Please give me peace within my soul.

The reader's response:

The reader should seek to study the Psalm as above, look at the response of the writer, then develop his or her own prayer, accordingly.

How are you like/unlike the Psalmist?

____

What is your response to the Psalm?

____

____

What is your prayer?

____

____

Psalm 21

Truth — The Psalmist thanks his Lord for His care. He states that God "answers the longing" of his heart. Clearly nothing or no one, other than the Lord could do this.

Issues and Points — Only God is able, and in His love, God does help.

Effect on the Psalmist — He is full of praise and worship for his God.

How am I unlike the Psalmist — I must confess that I am not always full of praise and worship for my great God. In fact, quite often I am so carried away by activities and needs that God is not central in my thoughts. This I must confess, also.

My response — To confess, to give thanks and to praise my God for loving me so.

My Prayer:

Lord, I don't know why You help me so,
Why You care for such a one as I,
But though I don't understand Your love,
I accept it without knowing the why.
And yet, as simple as my mind may be,
It grasps that You do care for me.
And though I don't deserve Your love,
I thank You for so loving me.

The reader's response:

How are you like/unlike the Psalmist?

____

What is your response to the Psalm?

____

____

What is your prayer?

____

____

Psalm 42

Truth — The writer finds himself far away, geographically, from the place where he worshiped his God. But distance can be in heart and in spirit as well. Only the renewed joy of God's presence and His peace will satisfy.

Issues and points — The believer must not only recognize his plight, being far from his God, but call out to God to restore him.

Effect on the Psalmist — He cries out in one of the sweetest cries in the Psalms: "As the deer pants for water, so my soul longs for You, Oh Lord."

How am I like/unlike the Psalmist? When I recognize the cause of my heart ache and cry out to God He refreshes me, but often I remain in my misery without calling out to Him.

My response — To cry out to the Lord with the Psalmist.

My prayer:
Lord, I would be with You,
My soul thirsts to be by Your side.
How could any earthly desire compare?
You are the God of all creation,
You are the preserver of my soul,
How could anyone ever compare?
In my trouble I think of You,
Such thoughts are fresh and exciting
As water cascading over the fall,
So, even then, Your grace is all I need.

The reader's response:

How are you like/unlike the Psalmist?

____

What is your response to the Psalm?

____

____

What is your prayer?

____

____

Psalm 55

Truth — The Psalmist is betrayed by a friend (as was Christ).

Issues and points — The Psalmist groans at the injustice and treachery.

Effect on the Psalmist — Initially he wants God's retribution, but slowly he yields to the love and mercy of his great God.

How am I unlike the Psalmist? I, too, have *complained* over injustice against me, but unlike the Psalmist, I haven't totally turned it over to the Lord so that I might rejoice in Him.

My response — Forgive me, Lord, and cause me to ever rejoice in Your goodness and mercy.

My prayer:

What rejoicing I have in my soul,
That my great God considers me.
For when I ask, He hears, and answers,
And opens His ear to my plea.
Though I am small, weak and impure,
He still reaches down to me.
When troubles cause me to fear,
Then He reaches down to me.
What could I do if I didn't praise Him
For He keeps reaching down to me.

The reader's response:

How are you like/unlike the Psalmist?

____

What is your response to the Psalm?

____

____

What is your prayer?

Psalm 23

Truth — The Psalmist looked totally to the Lord as his Shepherd.

The Issues and points — His needs, his rest, his refreshing, his protection, his food all came from the hand of the loving Shepherd, Who was also his God and King.

Effect on the Psalmist — He never had to want.

How am I unlike the Psalmist? I do not have complete and total trust, at all times, in my great God and Savior.

My response — Lord I am so foolish in failing to trust in You completely.

My prayer:

Lord, I am so dumb,
I don't know when to rest, or even eat,
I forget how good Your comfort is,
I forget that You will guide me aright.
Thank You for being so gracious and kind,
Thank You for loving me, a sinner,
Thank You for bringing me into Your home
I don't understand, but thank You, Lord.

The reader's response:

How are you like/unlike the Psalmist?

____

What is your response to the Psalm?

____

____

What is your prayer?

____

____

Psalm 37

Truth — Only the Lord does fully satisfy.

Issues and points — Evildoers have a certain and unhappy end but those who trust in the Lord will be established.

Effect on the Psalmist — He becomes an encourager and guide to others as he explains the goodness and protection of the Lord.

How am I unlike the Palmist — How amazing for the Psalmist to become an evangelist in the middle of his praise to God. I confess I do not do this.

My response — Forgive me, Lord, for not being concerned about and not loving all that You do love.

My prayer:

Why should I, how could I
Seek happiness away from You, Lord?
All in this world, all in this life,
passes as vapor or grass in the field,
Appearing, only to be gone.
But You, Oh Lord, are forever,
Your goodness is without end,
Your mercy is never failing,
Your joy unspeakable.
Cause me to know and love You,
Without Your strength, I will surely fall.
The reader's response:

How are you like/unlike with the Psalmist?

____

What is your response to the Psalm?

____

____

What is your prayer?

____

____

Psalm 43

Truth — The Believer ought never to be cast down.

Issues and points — God judges and defends us, He Rescues us, He is our stronghold, He is merciful, He is Truth, and gives us great joy.

Effect on the Psalmist — He asks his own soul why be cast down for God is both Lord and Savior.

How am I unlike the Psalmist — Often, when troubles seem beyond me, I am not as trusting in my great God as he was. It's not that I don't know He loves me and that He will take care of me, but still, I have fears within me.

My response — Lord, I confess that even as I trust You, fears spring up in time of trouble. Take these away by Your grace, Lord.

My prayer:

Lord, You are always my defender,
You always know my needs,
You want the very best for me,
Why, then, should I be cast down?
I do not trust enough,
I have not confessed and forsaken all my sins,
I have not turned over my life to You, Lord,
I now bow and confess and give You thanks.

The reader's response:

How are you like/unlike with the Psalmist?

____

What is your response to the Psalm?

____

____

What is your prayer?

____

____

Psalm 44

Truth — Our holy God cannot look upon sin, but He has provided a way to bring us to Himself.

Issues and points — God did great works for His children in times past, but now He seems afar off. The Psalmist forgets the promises the Children of Israel made back to the Lord and sees only that his God is silent.
Effect on the Psalmist — He cries out to his God to return and save and help because He is a God of lovingkindness.

How am I like the Psalmist — How often do I cry out for God's help and protection, forgetting that I, too, have sinned and have not turned those sins completely over to Him and depended totally upon His grace and His mercy.

My response — Forgive me, Lord, for not coming as a clean vessel to You by first praising You and then confessing all of my sins before asking for Your help.

My prayer:

In good times we praise Your Name, Oh Lord,
For that is quite easy to do.
But in bad times when You cannot be found,
We forget to come as clean vessels first.
Now, Lord, we fall on our knees,
We confess our sins and plead Your grace,
We have naught else to please You,
Only Your mercy saves — only Your mercy.
Lord, You may bring us low,
And as we trust, You then bring us up to You.

The reader's response:

How are you like/unlike with the Psalmist?

____

What is your response to the Psalm?

____

____

What is your prayer?

____

____

Psalm 62

Truth — The Psalmist cries out, "My hope is in the Lord."

Issues and Points — The Psalmist is in great peril, but, in his God he is calm.

Effect on the Psalmist — He is at peace in the midst of strife.

How am I unlike the Psalmist — Often, in trouble, I do not just rest in my Beloved.

My response — I need to be at peace and show that peace to those without the Lord.

My prayer:

I wait patiently for the Lord,
He is my salvation.
I trust in Him,
For He is my salvation.
My hope is in Him,
Because He is my salvation.
My deliverance is from Him,
Yes, He truly is my salvation.

The reader's response:

How are you like/ unlike with the Psalmist?

____

What is your response to the Psalm?

____

____

What is your prayer?

____

____

Psalm 63

Truth — The Psalmist needs his Lord and seeks Him early.

Issues and Points — He is parched and dry and needs the refreshment of a loving and caring Heavenly Father.

Effect on the Psalmist — In this Psalm we see the Psalmist begin in thirst for his God and continuing with blessing and peace.

How am I unlike the Psalmist — Many times I have not rushed to my heavenly Father on my knees and in tears as did the Psalmist.

My response — Oh God, by your great grace and love, cause me to rush to You for all my needs.

My prayer:

My soul thirsts for You,
My body aches for You,
I am not complete without You,
You are my God, oh Lord.
I need You,
I long for You,
I love You,
You are my God, oh Lord.

The reader's response:

How are you like/unlike with the Psalmist?

____

What is your response to the Psalm?

____

____

What is your prayer?

____

____

Psalm 75

Truth — This is another Psalm which is entirely about God, His Name, His righteousness, and His judgment.

Issues and Points — God is in charge, whether man recognizes it or not.

Effect on the Psalmist — The Psalmist is determined to make his Lord known to others.
How am I unlike the Psalmist? I confess that, many times, do not make my great and loving Lord known to men.

My response — Oh Lord, cause me to tell of Your greatness.

My prayer:

Lord, I give You thanks for being my God,
And always taking care of me.
For although I trip, and stumble and fall,
You lift me up and I give You thanks.
You alone are worthy and able to judge,
You raise one up and put down another,
And in all You do, You are holy,
And for this, Lord, I give You thanks.

The reader's response:

How are you like/unlike with the Psalmist?

____

What is your response to the Psalm?

____

____

What is your prayer?

____

____

Reader's Note on Chapter 2 — In all of these Psalms, God is in charge and each Psalm is about Him. Our responsibility, then, is to pray for His being in charge of our heart as well.

Chapter 3
God's Mercy Toward the Psalmist and the Reader/Believer

The following eight Psalms stress the wonderful mercy of God.

Psalm 136

Truth — God's mercy, echoed in every truth, endures forever.

Issues and points — The Psalmist does not want to forget how everlasting is God's mercy.

Effect on the Psalmist — He begins with the great miracles of God, then ends by rejoicing that his God remembers the Psalmist's people, and that He saves and provides as well.

How am I unlike the Psalmist? I need to confess that this truth is not always reflected in my life.

My response — Lord, cause me to constantly affirm, in my heart, Your everlasting mercy to me.

My prayer:

No matter what I consider about You, Lord,
Your mercy endures forever.
And though You are the God of creation,
Your mercy endures forever, for me.
Although You have done so much for Your own,
Still, Your mercy endures forever.
Bring me constantly to my knees,
For Your mercy endures forever for me.

The reader's response:

How are you like/unlike with the Psalmist?

____

What is your response to the Psalm?

____

____

What is your prayer?

____

____

Psalm 139

Truth — God knows everything about the Psalmist, yet He loves me.

Issues and points — He is Creator, Sustainer, Redeemer, and our loving and merciful, all-knowing God.

Effect on the Psalmist — He is only able to cry out, "My Lord, I don't understand Your love and power and grace to me."

How am I unlike the Psalmist? I do not consider the greatness of my Lord and His wonderful caring for me.

My response — Forgive me, Lord, forgive me!

My prayer:

You know all about me, Lord,
And yet You still love me.
Before I was born, You were there,
Before You is my soul laid bare.
You know all about me, Lord,
And yet You still love me.

The reader's response:

How are you like/unlike with the Psalmist?

____

What is your response to the Psalm?

____

____

What is your prayer?

____

____

Psalm 66

Truth — God saves us because of His grace and mercy.

Issues and points — We should continually thank our God and praise Him.

Effect on the Psalmist — He keeps his vows to His Lord.

How am I unlike the Psalmist — I have not vowed as he did.

My response — Lord, as the Psalmist cried out to You in keeping his vows, Lord, by Your grace, I will, I will, too.

My prayer:

Thank You Lord, for showing mercy
For without it I am lost.
I dare not come to You,
Except for Your mercy and grace.
You could refuse my prayer,
You could judge me after my sins.
What hope, then would I have,
To come to You, my holy God?
But Lord, You did not refuse Your mercy,
So that now I am able to live with You.

The reader's response:

How are you like/unlike with the Psalmist?

____

What is your response to the Psalm?

____

What is your prayer?

Psalm 48

Truth — God, in His love, takes care of His children.

Issues and points — God defended His children and protected them.

Effect on the Psalmist — He is amazed at the greatness of God's mercy.

How am I unlike the Psalmist? I so often forget how merciful He is to me.

My response — Lord, I am overwhelmed by Your mercy.

My prayer:

The God of the universe cares for me,
He, Who is mighty and worthy of praise,
Whose Name is known in all creation,
Has shown mercy to a sinner like me.

The reader's response:

How are you like/unlike with the Psalmist?

What is your response to the Psalm?

____

____

What is your prayer?

____

____

Psalm 67

Truth — God is worthy of all reverence, yet He is merciful.

Issues and points — We need to always praise Him.

Effect on the Psalmist — He is full of thanksgiving for his God.

How am I unlike the Psalmist? I get so caught up with this world that I fail to thank Him for His mercy.

My response — Lord, cause me to remember Your mercy.

My prayer:

Lord, I ask You for mercy and blessing,
For I have no other hope.
Lord, I pray that Your radiance shines on me,
For without You, I do not know the way.
Oh, that everyone would praise Your Name,
For You, alone, are worthy.
May all give You reverence,
For You, Lord, alone, are worthy.

The reader's response:

How are you like/unlike with the Psalmist?

____

What is your response to the Psalm?

____

____

What is your prayer?

____

____

Psalm 100

Truth — God's mercy is everlasting.

Issues and points — He is God, He is good, and His faithfulness extends to all generations.

Effect on the Psalmist — He rejoices and sings to his great God.

How am I unlike the Psalmist — I often do not rejoice in my Lord.

My response — Forgive me, Lord, and cause me to rejoice only in You.

My prayer:

Lord, the day will come,
When all peoples will serve You,
When all will be sheep in Your pasture,

Because Your mercy is everlasting.
Lord, You are so good,
Your faithfulness is forever,
You are so good,
And Your mercy is everlasting.

The reader's response:

How are you like/unlike with the Psalmist?

____

What is your response to the Psalm?

____

____

What is your prayer?

____

____

Psalm 106

Truth — God is always merciful to His own.

Issues and points — God loves us even as we sin, He cares while we are far from Him, and He hears and restores us to Himself.

Effect on the Psalmist-He believed his God, he remembered how his people disobeyed the Lord, but He saved them.

How am I unlike the Psalmist? I do not often consider how great in mercy God has been to His own and to me.

My response — Forgive me, Lord and lead me in Your Will.

My prayer:

I thank You, Lord, for Your mercy,
You loved me, even as I sinned.
You cared, even as I was far from You,
You are so good and merciful to me.
Lord, when You saw my distress,
When You heard my cries of grief,
You had compassion because of Your grace.
Yes, You are so merciful to me.
The reader's response:

How are you like/unlike with the Psalmist?

____

What is your response to the Psalm?

____

____

What is your prayer?

____

____

Psalm 118

Truth — Although God is Omnipotent, He is also all merciful.

Issues and points — The Psalmist cried out to God in his distress and his Lord set him free.

Effect on the Psalmist — He wants all Israel to shout with him about how God's mercy endures forever.

How am I unlike the Psalmist? Not only have I not cried out for others to praise Him with me, but I don't thank Him enough.

My response — Break me and mold me according to Your will.

My prayer:

You are the only true God,
There is no other,
Your deeds are beyond comparison,
Your holiness unattainable.
I do not understand Your mighty power,
I can only receive Your love.
Unless You had saved me, I would still be lost,
But Your mercy came down to even me, Lord.

The reader's response:

How are you like/unlike with the Psalmist?

____

What is your response to the Psalm?

____

____

What is your prayer?

____

____

Chapter 4
Learning Who Our God Is

Twenty-four Psalms help us, specifically, to understand more about our great God. These are 28, 33, 72, 145, 2, 11, 26, 36, 45, 47, 58, 60, 76, 89, 93, 99, 104, 110, 111, 113, 114, 123, 129, 144. By studying how the Psalmist approached God we will learn more about praying to Him.

Psalm 28

Truth — there is only one God, and only He is able to hear us.

Issues and points — Unless his God hears and answers, the Psalmist is as one on the brink of the pit. Others do not trust God, but the Psalmist does.

Effect on the Psalmist — God answers and the Psalmist is rejoicing.

How am I unlike the Psalmist — I don't cry enough for my God to hear and answer me.

My response — Cause me, Oh Lord, never to question You and never to cease to call on You.

My prayer:

Lord, I call, pouring me heart out to You,
Pleading for Your answer to my prayer.

Without Your response I am as dead,
Nothing else in this life has value.
There is even a graver issue, Lord,
Who could answer should You refuse?
Who has Your power, Your love, Your grace?
No one, no, no one, who could sit in Your place.
Thank You Lord for Your steadfast love,
Thank You for caring for me.
You respond at just the right time,
You reach down to help me in my need.

The reader's response:

How are you like/unlike with the Psalmist?

____

What is your response to the Psalm?

____

____

What is your prayer?

____

____

Psalm 33

Truth — Our God is beyond description, or measure.

Issues and points — We need to praise Him, learn more about Him from His Word, seeking to do all He would have us to do and trust totally in Him.

Effect on the Psalmist — He trusts Him and His mercy.

How am I unlike the Psalmist — I do not always wholly trust Him.

My response — Lord, cause me, by Your mercy and grace, to trust always in You.

My prayer:

How presumptuous to pretend to know God
To do so implies we are the same.
I cannot profane, but I can give You thanks,
For You, Lord, are holy and most worthy.
Let me list, in human terms,
What You showed to me:
Your power, truth, righteousness,
Your love grace, care,
Your kindness, Your forgiveness,
And Your mercy, Your great mercy.
I bow, I repent, I plead Your mercy,
Submitting myself wholly to You.

The reader's response:

How are you like/unlike with the Psalmist?

____

What is your response to the Psalm?

____

____

What is your prayer?

———————————————————————

———————————————————————

Psalm 72

Truth — God always does what is right.

Issues and points — God provides righteousness, and the king asks for His complete direction and control.

Effect on the Psalmist — He calls to his God for wisdom and he wants to praise Him.

How am I unlike the Psalmist — I do not ask, enough, for His wisdom.

My response — Lord, I need Your grace and Your wisdom.

My prayer:

Lord, when I call on You for help,
When my prayers are very specific,
I am at peace, knowing fully
That You are always righteous.
When I pray for one of Your own,
When I give a list of needs,
I still know You accept me,
For You, Lord, are ever righteous.
Forgive me and receive me, Lord,
For You, alone, are righteous.

The reader's response:

How are you like/unlike with the Psalmist?

____

What is your response to the Psalm?

____

____

What is your prayer?

____

____

Psalm 145 .

Truth — God is always and ever worthy

Issues and points — God's works, His goodness, His righteousness, His mercy, His power, and His Name are ever worthy.

Effect on the Psalmist — He praises God's Name, His works, His glory and majesty, His goodness, His mercy, His faithfulness, and His watchcare.

How am I unlike the Psalmist — I do not praise my God enough or about all of His attributes.

My response — Forgive me Lord, for slighting Your greatness and majesty.

My prayer:

I exalt, praise, glorify and magnify You, oh Lord,
You are ever worthy of praise.

And were I to continue for all time,
Your greatness would still have no end.
I bow down, I confess
Do save me by Your grace.

The reader's response:

How are you like/unlike with the Psalmist?

____

What is your response to the Psalm?

____

____

What is your prayer?

____

____

Psalm 2

Truth — Although our God is sovereign and holy, not all recognize Him as God.

Issues and points — Men fail to recognize His sovereignty, and they seek to rebel against Him.

Effect on the Psalmist — His faith is rewarded by being a listener to the conversation between the Father and the Son.

How am I unlike the Psalmist — Although I am not a listener, I rejoice in the grace He has shown to me.

My response — Thank You, Lord, for loving me so.

My prayer:

That man should hate You is hard to understand
For all the good given from Your hand.
And though You are omnipotent
You receive me, a poor sinful man.
You, Lord, placed Your Son on the throne
He is my Savior, He calls me His own.
Thank You, Lord, for loving me so,
Thank You for being willing to make me whole.

The reader's response:

How are you like/unlike with the Psalmist?

____

What is your response to the Psalm?

____

____

What is your prayer?

____

____

Psalm 11

Truth — God, our righteous God, is in His holy place.

Issues and points — Our righteous God is displeased with the wicked, and, He loves the upright.

Effect on the Psalmist — He rejoices in the righteousness of his great God.

How am I unlike the Psalmist — How often have I failed to rejoice in my God's righteousness.

My response — Forgive me Lord, for You are ever worthy.

My prayer:

To know my God is righteous
Brings great joy to my soul.
It tells me, He is not inconstant,
Being neither impulsive or changeable,
For He is ever faithful in His love to me.
My God is both holy and good,
He has no evil at all,
And what comfort this brings to my soul.
Yet He is omnipotent as well,
No one, no, nothing could remove Him from me.
And still, He is perfect in His love,
While loving even sinful me.
He removed my sin and gave me His life,
I could never love Him in kind,
But I must show Him by my life,
The thankfulness I have in my heart.

The reader's response:

How are you like/unlike with the Psalmist?

____

What is your response to the Psalm?

____

What is your prayer?

Psalm 26

Truth — The Psalmist asks his God to declare him righteous because of his heart.

Issues and points — The Psalmist trusts his God, he asks God to examine him, and he lives by faith.

Effect on the Psalmist — He declares, "I know He answers me!"

How am I unlike the Psalmist — Often I do not have the joy of my faith as does the Psalmist.

My response — Oh Lord, cause me, by Your grace, to have constant joy because You have so loved me.

My prayer:

Lord, I confess You as Lord and Savior
You have ever been holy and pure.
Thank You for causing me to trust You,
Thank You for declaring me righteous.
There was nothing I could do,
To become holy as You require,
But by faith, You made me so,
And by faith I believe it is so.
Cause me to praise You to all I meet
That they, too, may know of love and grace.

The reader's response:

How are you like/unlike with the Psalmist?

____

What is your response to the Psalm?

____

____

What is your prayer?

____

____

Psalm 36

Truth — God's mercy, faithfulness, holiness, judgments, and lovingkindness are unsearchable.

. Issues and points — The ungodly, however, do not consider God in this way.

Effect on the Psalmist — He is overcome by the wonder of the goodness and love of God.

How am I unlike the Psalmist? I am seldom overcome by God's mercy and holiness as is the Psalmist.

My response — Forgive me, Lord, and turn me toward You continually.

My prayer:

Lord, Your mercy has no limits

Your faithfulness is as the sky,
Your holiness as the mountains,
For You are so precious to me.
Your judgments are beyond understanding,
Yet Your love reaches out to all men,
Your holiness and Your law do agree,
For You are righteous wholly.
I plead only Your love and grace,
Continue to give me Your security.

The reader's response:

How are you like/unlike with the Psalmist?

____

What is your response to the Psalm?

____

____

What is your prayer?

____

____

Psalm 45

Truth — Our Holy God loves us and brings us to Himself.

Issues and points — God is eternal, He is righteous, He loves holiness.

Effect on the Psalmist — His enthusiastic heart cause him to overflow with praise for his Lord.

How am I unlike the Psalmist — How often am I impoverished in my praise of God.

My response — Forgive me, Lord, for failing to praise You.

My prayer:

Lord, it is right to praise You,
You are both eternal and holy.
But what is most amazing
Is that You reached down to save me.
Why You do, I do not know,
Only that giving is part of Your loving,
And a loving God, we do understand,
So our only response, in faith, is praise.

The reader's response:

How are you like/unlike with the Psalmist?

____

What is your response to the Psalm?

____

____

What is your prayer?

____

____

Psalm 47

Truth — God is king of all the earth and He has provided for His own.

Issues and points — He chose the land and He has shown His power to His own.

Effect on the Psalmist — He rejoices at how good his God is.

How am I unlike the Psalmist — I often lose the blessing of rejoicing in my great God.

My response — Lord, cause me to rejoice in You.

My prayer:

Lord, I confess You as my God and Savior,
You have ever been holy and true.
Thank You for causing me to trust in You,
Thank You for giving me righteousness.
There was nothing I ever could do,
To become holy as You require,
Yet, by faith, I believe You made me so,
I thank You for bring it to pass.
Let me praise You to those I meet,
So others will know what You can do.

The reader's response:

How are you like/unlike with the Psalmist?

____

What is your response to the Psalm?

____

What is your prayer?

Psalm 58

Truth — Our God judges righteously.

Issues and points — Man, apart from God is full of evil, but God is always victorious.

Effect on the Psalmist — By recognizing God's holiness and power, he is able to commit evildoers over to Him.

How am I unlike the Psalmist — I often dwell on what should be done to those who are evil.

My response — Cause me, Lord, to turn everything over to You.

My prayer:

I cannot fault Your judgments, Lord,
Your decisions are all trustworthy.
There is never evil in what You do,
For You judge righteously.
But thank You, Lord, for Your grace,
For You are righteous and You also save.

The reader's response:

How are you like/unlike with the Psalmist?

What is your response to the Psalm?

____

____

What is your prayer?

____

____

Psalm 60

Truth — God gives us promises in His holiness, but we must confess and forsake our sin.

Issues and points — When we sin, God appears afar off, until we confess and forsake.

Effect on the Psalmist — He recognizes the need for him to confess.

How am I unlike the Psalmist — How often do I neglect to confess my sins to Him.

My response — Forgive me for not confessing, Lord.

My prayer:

Lord, dare I ask anything of You,
If I haven't asked forgiveness first?
Dare I even try to come to You,
Except it be by faith alone?
When will I truly understand,
How righteous and holy You are?
And only by faith, only by faith,

Dare I come, that is all I can give.
And when in faith I do confess and trust,
You, in Your grace, receive even me.

The reader's response:

How are you like/unlike with the Psalmist?

____

What is your response to the Psalm?

____

____

What is your prayer?

____

____

____

Psalm 76

Truth — God's glory is beyond comparison.

Issues and points — Men may defy God but every knee shall bow to Him.

Effect on the Psalmist — Lord, You are more glorious.

How am I unlike the Psalmist — How often I do not see how glorious my Lord really is.

My response — I cry out to You, my glorious God.

My prayer :

Lord, no matter what man lifts his hand,
Or what peoples seek to defy You,
All will bow in fear to You,
For You are more glorious.
When nations begin to plunder,
And kings become defiant,
Even they will face your judgment,
For You are more glorious.
Yet You loved me, You accepted me,
Now my heart knows You are more glorious.
The reader's response:

How are you like/unlike with the Psalmist?

What is your response to the Psalm?

What is your prayer?

Psalm 89

Truth — God is holy and beyond our understanding.

Issues and points — His faithfulness, His mercy, His promises, His greatness, His awesomeness, His power and His hatred of sin.

Effect on the Psalmist — He cries out to His God because he is far from Him, because of sin.

How am I like the Psalmist? How often is He far from me because of my sin?

My response — Forgive me Lord, for sinning, for not confessing, and for foolishly thinking that I could be close to You with unconfessed sin.

My prayer:

How wonderful to know Your greatness and love,
To experience Your heavenly praise,
But how sad, that right where I am,
Not everyone knows You as Lord.
Though You are infinite in power,
Though You are righteous and loving,
Though you are deserving of all worship,
Not everyone knows You as Lord.
In Your wisdom and grace,
Cause me to share You as my Lord,
For You are a most awesome God.
The reader's response:

How are you like/unlike with the Psalmist?

____

What is your response to the Psalm?

____

____

What is your prayer?

____

____

Psalm 93

Truth — Our Lord is always on the throne.

Issues and points — He is majestic, omnipotent, eternal, and holy.

Effect on the Psalmist — The Psalmist is full of praise for his Lord.

How am I unlike the Psalmist? I confess to not always being so aware of my great God and His love for me.

My response — Forgive me, Lord, for not always recognizing Your Holiness and Your Righteousness.

My prayer:

Whether I show it or even know it,
You, Lord, are on the throne.
There is none to move You,
From everlasting, You, alone, are God.
Cause me, Lord, to ever worship You,
And to proclaim, yes, to proclaim You, too!
The reader's response:

How are you like/unlike with the Psalmist?

____

What is your response to the Psalm?

____

What is your prayer?

Psalm 104

Truth — Man is unable to comprehend or describe God or His creation.

Issues and points — All that is in the universe has been created by an omniscient, omnipotent God. Man still does not understand God's greatness after thousands of years of analysis and study.

Effect on the Psalmist — He can only utter, "Praise the Lord, oh my soul!"

How am I unlike the Psalmist? How often do I forget to praise my great God.

My response — Forgive me, Lord, do forgive me.

My prayer:

Lord, how impertinent of me to speak at all,
Much less, seek to speak of things eternal.
All that I know is so limited, so small,
It could never measure eternity at all.
Were I to try to explain Your creation,
It would be from the inside, not out,
At what point in time and space,
Could I, puny I, circumscribe the all?
Lord, I only bow down to You,
Loving You and thanking You for Your grace.

The reader's response:

How are you like/unlike with the Psalmist?

____

What is your response to the Psalm?

____

____

What is your prayer?

____

____

Psalm 110

Truth — God, You are ever in charge.

Issues and points — Man, in his evil and foolishness, thinks to outwit or overcome God. How foolish and terrible are such wicked thoughts.

Effect on the Psalmist — He sees into the future and tells us what our holy and omnipotent God will do.

How am I unlike the Psalmist? God has not allowed me to see as does the Psalmist, but He has enabled me to trust Him.

My response — Lord, I can thank You for loving me.

My prayer:

How strange, Lord, that man might plot
And think he would overthrow You?

You make all Your enemies a footstool,
For You are ever in charge.
Those that love You, prosper
They are dressed in the beauty of holiness,
For You, Who cannot lie, said it,
And You, oh Lord, are ever in charge.

The reader's response:

How are you like/unlike with the Psalmist?

____

What is your response to the Psalm?

____

____

What is your prayer?

____

____

Psalm 111

Truth — We can know no truth, save He Who is Truth.

Issues and points — His deeds and His works are great. His righteousness, and mercy, and power, and precepts, and redemption and His Name are beyond our understanding.

Effect on the Psalmist — He praises God with all his heart.

How am I unlike the Psalmist? I do not continually praise my great God and Savior.

My response — Forgive me, Lord, for not always praising You with all my heart.

My prayer:

Lord, You are worthy of praise,
Your works and promises are great,
Your mercy and grace, they last forever,
I am greatly in awe of You.
You are righteous and holy,
Even Your Name is to be revered,
I understand, as I obey
My wisdom begins as I am in awe of You.

The reader's response:

How are you like/unlike with the Psalmist?

____

What is your response to the Psalm?

____

____

What is your prayer?

____

____

Psalm 113

Truth — You, alone, are worthy, Lord.

Issues and points — Praise God and His Name for none could be compared to Him.

Effect on the Psalmist — He cries for all to praise the Lord.

How am I like the Psalmist? I, too, have to cry out to my gracious Lord and to praise Him.

My response — Even when I praise Him, I do not always ask others to praise Him, too.

My prayer:

Lord, I need to sing Your praises,
To acknowledge Your Name is blessed,
To rejoice that You are full of glory,
And that You, Lord, are worthy.
You lift up the poor,
You care for the needy,
You even humble Yourself to visit me,
I love You, Lord, for You are ever worthy.

The reader's response:

How are you like/unlike with the Psalmist?

____

What is your response to the Psalm?

____

____

What is your prayer?

Psalm 114

Truth — Our omnipotent God has power beyond us.

Issues and points — God stops the seas, He parts the river, He shakes the mountains, for He, alone, is God.

Effect on the Psalmist — He asks, "Why did you shake, mountains, or, why did you divide, sea?"

How am I unlike the Psalmist? I am not close enough to my Lord to ask Him questions on tough subjects.

My response — I can't begin to understand the greatness of my Lord.

My prayer:

Lord, You are so very great,
I don't even begin to understand,
For the entire earth obeys You,
Such power is far beyond me.
How could the seas flee away,
How could the mountains move about?
 How could rock become water?
Your power is beyond me.
But I trust in You as Savior,
And by Your grace, You watch over me.

The reader's response:

How are you like/unlike with the Psalmist?

____

What is your response to the Psalm?

____

____

What is your prayer?

____

____

Psalm 123

Truth — God is far from us, until we worship Him.

Issues and points — We need to cry out for His mercy.

Effect on the Psalmist — He looks for God's mercy and he is overcome with shame for his sins.

How am I unlike the Psalmist — I am not often enough overcome with my sins and His holiness.

My response — Lord, show me Your Holiness and then cause me to bow down to Your greatness.

My prayer:

You dwell far above me, Lord,
Where I am not able to go.

But I can lift my eyes to You,
"Lord, tell me what to do."
I ask for Your mercy,
Because of Your grace.
I make no demands,
I fall down before You on my face.

The reader's response:

How are you like/unlike with the Psalmist?

____

What is your response to the Psalm?

____

____

What is your prayer?

____

____

Psalm 129

Truth — The Lord is ever righteous.

Issues and points — God protects His own and they praise Him.

Effect on the Psalmist — He calls out for all Israel to praise his great God.

How am I unlike the Psalmist? I don't call for all men to praise Him.

My response — Forgive my selfishness in not sharing, whenever I am able, Your Love and Grace.

My prayer:

Cause me to continue to look to You, Lord
And not to worry about men.
You do always lift up Your own,
So my enemies cannot harm me again.
But I must ever look to You,
I could never go alone.
You are my righteous Lord,
You ever protect me from the unknown.

The reader's response:

How are you like/unlike with the Psalmist?

____

What is your response to the Psalm?

____

____

What is your prayer?

____

____

Psalm 144

Truth — God is the Rock that all believers must cling to.

Issues and points — He instructs, He loves, He delivers, and He subdues.

Effect on the Psalmist — The Psalmist hides in his God and Lord.

How am I unlike the Psalmist? I do not seek, always, to hide in Him.

My response — How often do I seek my own strength, my own answers, when He wants to take care of me.

My prayer:

You protect me in so many ways,
My Rock, my Fortress, my Deliverer.
Why do You care about me,
Why do You even think about me?
I am but a breath,
Appearing only to be gone,
But in Your love, You rescued me,
I thank You, Lord, with all my heart.

The reader's response:

How are you like/unlike with the Psalmist?

What is your response to the Psalm?

What is your prayer?

____

____

Chapter 5
Learning That the Name of Our God Is Holy

Five Psalms emphasize the very holiness of God's Name: 30, 54, 68, 92, and 109. We will get a greater understanding of His holiness as we examine these Psalms.

Psalm 30

Truth — The saints are reminded to remember the holy Name of God.

Issues and points — The Psalmist calls out for the saints to sing unto the Lord for the many things He has done for the Psalmist.

Effect on the Psalmist — He praises his Lord for God not only heard his prayer but answered in a wonderful way.

How am I unlike the Psalmist? I do not always rejoice or rejoice with such fervor for what the Lord does for me.

My response — Forgive me, Lord, for being unthankful.

My prayer:

How arrogant, Lord, for us to utter Your Name,

How disdainful we are of Your glory.
For with whatever words we use to call on You,
With those very words we sin by shutting You in.
You are Creator of all that exists,
You are Sustainer of everything,
You cannot be limited, to do so is sin.
Forgive us Lord, forgive us.
We cannot know how truly great You are,
We can only bow, in worship, asking for Your mercy.

The reader's response:

How are you like/unlike with the Psalmist?

____

What is your response to the Psalm?

____

____

What is your prayer?

____

____

Psalm 54

Truth — God's true Name describes, as best we can understand, Who He is.

Issues and points — God saves by His Name, He preserves by His power, He supports and lifts up the Psalmist's soul.

Effect on the Psalmist — He cries out for his God to save him by His Name and he tells us all the great things his God has done for him.

How am I unlike the Psalmist? How many time I fail to cry out to my loving God, and how weak is my testimony of His love and great deeds toward me.

My response — Although I am thankful for what my great God has done for me, I need to know Him better, and I need to proclaim His love and grace to others.

My prayer:

Dare I even pronounce Your Name, Lord,
You, Who are above all creation
In Your power You set the universe in motion,
Your holiness is beyond understanding.
How dare I limit You,
For by using Your Name, I defile it.
Let me call out to You,
Let me trust only in Your mercy and Your grace.

The reader's response:

How are you like/unlike with the Psalmist?

What is your response to the Psalm?

____

____

What is your prayer?

____

____

Psalm 68

Truth — Our God and His Name are everlasting.

Issues and points — The Psalmist recounts many of God's gracious and merciful responses to His people who cry out to Him,

Effect on the Psalmist — He cries out "Sing unto the Lord," "May the Lord be blessed," "Our God is the God of deliverance," and many other joyous praises.

. How am I unlike the Psalmist — I am so wanting in my praise to Him.

My response — Forgive me Lord for my weak and unloving response to your great mercy to me.

My prayer:

Lord, how great is Your Name!
I can only worship You in fear,
I can only bow down in praise,
For Your Name is everlasting.
I do not begin to understand,
But I rejoice in Your grace,
And my weak efforts to reach to You,

Fail, until You reach down to me.
Lord, how very great is Your Name,
Your Name, alone, is everlasting.

The reader's response:

How are you like/unlike with the Psalmist?

____

What is your response to the Psalm?

____

____

What is your prayer?

____

____

Psalm 92

Truth — God's Name is worthy of all our thanks and praise.

Issues and points — God shows us His mercy, His faithfulness, His works, and He is our Rock.

Effect on the Psalmist — He thanks and praises His Lord for His goodness and for His great Name.

How am I unlike the Psalmist — How often I fail to rejoice in my God.

My response — I confess my selfishness and terrible sin in not praising and worshiping Him as I should.

My prayer:
Lord, let me tell of Your mercy in the morning,
Let me recount Your faithfulness at night.
For all that You do is awesome
And the depths of Your thoughts far beyond me.
I could not reach up to You,
You, in love, reached down to me.
Doing so in grace,
Forgiving and loving me.
And You did this all in righteousness,
My Lord, You are my Rock.

The reader's response:

How are you like/unlike with the Psalmist?

____

What is your response to the Psalm?

____

____

What is your prayer?

____

Psalm 109

Truth — The Lord does deal with His own, according to His Name.

Issues and points — The Psalmist recounts the many troubles brought upon him by the wicked. But after telling his Lord, he leaves their future with his God. He is then able to rejoice in His God.

Effect on the Psalmist — He separates his worship from the pressures around him and does not stain that worship by continuing to fret about those who seek to harm him.

How am I unlike the Psalmist? I do not always leave such issues with Him and, therefore my worship is sullied.

My response — Forgive me, Lord, do, I pray, forgive me.

My prayer:

You are holy and righteous
And there is no one like You, Lord.
Do save me because You are righteous,
Do deal with me according to Your Name.
Do help me, oh my Lord and my God,
For I am weak, sinful, and needy,
My heart is broken within me,
Do deal with me according to Your Name.

The reader's response:

How are you like/unlike with the Psalmist?

____

What is your response to the Psalm?

____

____

What is your prayer?

____

____

Chapter 6
Learning That God's Word, His Judgments, and His Promises Are Holy

There are six Psalms (12, 19, 83, 94, 108, and 119) which are totally about His Word, and His Judgments and His Promises. Because God, Himself, is holy, then it follows that whatever He says is also holy.

Psalm 12

Truth — God's Word is both perfect and holy.

Issues and points — The Psalmist cries out for his God to rescue the oppressed and he reminds God of His promise to protect.

Effect on the Psalmist — He cries out in faith and hope in his great God.

How am I unlike the Psalmist — When everything looks bleak, I do not always have the strong hope that the Psalmist exhibits.

My response — God forgive me for my unbelief.

My prayer:

How comforting to know that God is true,
That His Words are already settled in heaven.
For it is impossible for Him to lie,

For He is our holy and righteous God.
Every Word that He speaks
Will surely come to pass
For He is both holy and omnipotent.
When He promises to help me,
I can know that He surely will.
When He promises to forgive me,
I have already been forgiven.
When He promises to save me,
He has already made me His child.
Oh my loving and gracious God,
Thank You for loving even me.

The reader's response:

How are you like/unlike with the Psalmist?

____

What is your response to the Psalm?

____

____

What is your prayer?

____

____

Psalm 19

Truth — His Law and His Word are always perfect.

Issues and points — All of creation declares and affirms God's glory. And His Word and His Truth act to quicken the soul of man and bring joy to his heart.

Effect on the Psalmist — God's holiness, in His Word, serves to bring the Psalmist closer to his God and Savior.

How am I unlike the Psalmist? God's Word is not always effective in my life because of unconfessed sin.

My response — Forgive me, Lord, for my hidden sins and cause me to rejoice in Your Word.

My prayer:

Lord, what does Your Law show to us?
But that You are a just and holy God.
And all we need to know about Your goodness
Can be seen in Its demands.
Our heart confirms Your Word is right,
And we dare not argue with Your Truth.
We need to accept Your Truth with joy,
But, Lord, our own sin gets in the way.
Yet when we follow and obey Your Word,
How happy we become,
For when within Your perfect will,
Then, You, in love, enable us to obey.

The reader's response:

How are you like/unlike with the Psalmist?

What is your response to the Psalm?

____

____

What is your prayer?

____

____

Psalm 83

Truth — Our God is holy and His judgments holy, too.

Issues and points — We need, in faith, to commit His enemies to Him.

Effect on the Psalmist — The Psalmist is obedient and at peace.

How am I unlike the Psalmist-How difficult to turn enemies over to Him and then be at peace.

My response — Lord, cause me to know how holy and yet how loving you are. Cause me to commit everything and everyone to You.

My prayer:

Lord, when I ask You to judge sinners,
I cannot exclude myself.
For You did judge me, and I confessed,
I repented and then You forgave me.
But, Lord, many still oppose You,
Many deny or defy Your rule.
But as You judge them righteously,

Some, Lord, will then turn to You.
Isn't that evidence, Lord,
That Your judgments are ever truth.

The reader's response:

How are you like/unlike with the Psalmist?

____

What is your response to the Psalm?

____

____

What is your prayer?

____

____

Psalm 94

Truth — Our God is both just and merciful.

Issues and points — Men openly sin against God and go against the Psalmist, also.

Effect on the Psalmist — He, in faith, turns everything over to his God and is at peace.

How am I unlike the Psalmist? I don't always turn everything over to Him and I am often not at peace about the activities of this life.

My response — Lord, forgive me and break me. Then cause me to trust wholly in You.

My prayer:

Although You are always just, Lord,
Your grace brings You down to me.
Under justice, I can claim nothing at all,
But, by grace, You gave so much to me.
When I fall, You pick me up,
When near death, You lift me up.
For though You are ever just, Lord,
By grace, You show mercy to me.

The reader's response

How are you like/unlike with the Psalmist?

____

What is your response to the Psalm?

____

____

What is your prayer?

____

____

Psalm 108

Truth — God promises to us in His holiness.

Issues and points — The Psalmist is able to rejoice in what God has done and will do, even though, at times the Psalmist does not see the carrying out of God's power.

Effect on the Psalmist — Even in trouble and uncertainty, he is at rest in trusting what his God is and will do.

How am I unlike the Psalmist — How often do I cry out because I have not seen His answer to my prayer or need.

My response — Forgive me, Lord, and by Your grace cause me to trust totally in You.

My prayer:

I am confident in You, Lord,
I sing from the depths of my soul.
I give You thanks before others,
For what You did promise in Your holiness.
Your mercy goes beyond the universe,
Your truth surrounds all space,
You do deliver me from all evil,
For so You promised in Your holiness.

The reader's response:

How are you like/unlike with the Psalmist?

____

What is your response to the Psalm?

____

____

What is your prayer?

Psalm 119

Truth — The Psalmist, records in many ways, how holy and perfect are the Words of God.

Issues and points — The Psalmist, in 22 groups, following the Hebrew alphabet, describes the righteousness and holiness of God's Word. His Word gives peace, instruction, salvation, life. and more.

Effect on the Psalmist — He is full of reverence and praise to His God.

How am I unlike the Psalmist? Lord, my faith, compared to that of the Psalmist is so beggarly and weak.

My response — Forgive me, Lord, do forgive me.

My prayer:

Lord, You did so love us,
That You shared with us Your Truth,
You made it simple, if we but yield,
For Your Spirit illumines our hearts.
Why do You love us so?
Why did You bother with us at all?
Was it because You cared and loved us,
And that You wanted to save us from our fall?
Keep us in Your Word, Lord,
Only by it do we keep close to You.

The reader's response:

How are you like/unlike with the Psalmist?

____

What is your response to the Psalm?

____

____

What is your prayer?

____

____

Chapter 7
God Loves Me

Perhaps the most amazing truth in the entire Psalms, in fact, in the Bible itself, is the truth that a perfect, eternal, holy, righteous, truthful, omnipotent God should love man, in general, and me in particular. Only by faith in Him and in His Son's provision for me am I able to see, ever so dimly, that my God does love me. He loves me, even though He knows everything about me, what is in my thoughts, my doubts, and my actions. Seven Psalms are directly concerned with God's love for me: 8, 25, 34, 56, 103, 137, and 147.

Psalm 8

Truth — Although God is majestic and full of glory, He reaches down in His grace to man, and even to the Psalmist.

Issues and points — The Psalmist begins a recitation of the qualities and activities of God, only to conclude that His very Name is majestic.

Effect on the Psalmist — He is in awe that such a glorious God would condescend to remember man, to visit him, and to make him just lower than God, Himself.

How am I unlike the Psalmist? I do not recognize the true holiness and majesty of my great God.

My response — My God, forgive me for not being in awe of You and Your holiness.

My prayer:

Our God is a great and mighty God
He is deserving of all our praise.
Soon all that is will honor Him,
Not yet, but precisely at His time.
Why should He not receive His due?
Why should not all men worship Him?
For His love is always at work,
Calling, in grace, to those who are lost.
Yet all have not yet honored Him,
And, if not, what hope is left?
Who else is both sovereign and love?
Who else cares for their souls?

The reader's response:

How are you like/unlike with the Psalmist?

____

What is your response to the Psalm?

____

____

What is your prayer?

____

____

Psalm 25

Truth — God's grace and mercy are beyond our understanding.

Issues and points — His guiding, His teaching, His faithfulness, His redemption, His righteousness, His mercy, His caring and His protection flow from His grace.

Effect on the Psalmist — He is humbled, but rejoicing in his God.

How am I unlike the Psalmist — I know God is a God of mercy and grace, but I forget it so often in my daily walk.

My response — Forgive me, Lord, Just forgive me.

My prayer:

Lord, You Who are sovereign and holy,
You did reach down to save even me.
Why would a holy God do this for me?
Why should He pardon and care for me?
Who am I to deserve Your love?
I know my weaknesses, but not as You
I know my sins, but not as You
I even know my sinful nature but not as You.
Without comparing Who You are and how low I am,
You cared, You watched over, You shared with me.
Thank You Lord for being so great,
Thank You for reaching down to me.
My prayers are broken up by tears
Because my gracious Lord has rescued me.

The reader's response:

How are you like/unlike with the Psalmist?

What is your response to the Psalm?

____

____

____

Psalm 34

Truth — God's love for us is beyond our comprehension.

Issues and points — The Psalmist prayed and God answered. He never disappoints, He is good, His children will never be in want, He withholds no good from those who love Him, and He redeems all who trust in Him.

Effect on the Psalmist — He praises his God always.

How am I unlike the Psalmist — Just to read that the Psalmist praises his God continuously puts me to shame and onto my knees.

My response — My God and Savior, I am so unthankful for Your love. Forgive me, forgive me, do forgive me.

My prayer:

How do I tell someone of Your love for me?
For You have surely answered my prayers,
And You deliver and protect me in life's way,
Providing only what is best for me.
But then, You are close and You listen,
You always listen when I walk with You.

But I still do not know why You love me so,
I don't understand that at all.
But Your Word and Your Spirit have witnessed to me,
My heart has the assurance of Your call,
So, though I don't understand, I trust,
Resting, because You, my God am also my Lord.

The reader's response:

How are you like/unlike with the Psalmist?

____

What is your response to the Psalm?

____

____

What is your prayer?

____

____

Psalm 56

Truth — God is so gracious that He loves even me.

Issues and points — God knows the Psalmist and his wanderings and He is always with him.

Effect on the Psalmist — He wants, always, to walk before his God in His Light.

How am I unlike the Psalmist? How often and how long do I fail to want to walk in God's light?

My response — Again, I can only bow and pray, "Forgive me, Lord, do forgive."

My prayer:

My Lord knows me and He still loves me,
Such grace I do not understand.
I am always able to lean on Him
Whenever troubles threaten to harm me.
I trust Him without fear,
For He knows me and He still loves me.
I am not afraid of death,
For He knows me and He still loves me.
Cause me, Lord, to tell others of Your love,
So that they, too, may come to You.

The reader's response:

How are you like/unlike with the Psalmist?

____

What is your response to the Psalm?

____

____

What is your prayer?

____

____

Psalm 103

Truth — God's love is shown to us in so many ways and with so many blessings.

Issues and points — God never forgets His benefits, He forgives all our sins, He heals all our sufferings, He surrounds us with kindness and mercy, and He satisfies our spirit with the good.

Effect on the Psalmist — He wants to thank his God with everything within him.

How am I unlike the Psalmist — The Psalmist's clear statement to His God that He wanted to thank Him with everything within him brought shame to my heart.

My response — Again, Lord, I can only ask for forgiveness and Your power to enable me to thank You with all that is within me.

My prayer:

Lord, if I try to tell what You have done for me
It is not enough, it is never enough.
For You forgive, You heal, You rescue me,
You surround me and satisfy my soul.
But for You, that is not enough,
For what You do is based on Who You are,
And my feeble attempts to describe You,
Would be sinning, not loving You.
You are so mighty, You are so great,
That my thanks and praise could never be enough.

The reader's response:

How are you like/unlike with the Psalmist?

What is your response to the Psalm?

____

____

What is your prayer?

____

____

Psalm 137

Truth — You love us wherever we are, Lord.

Issues and points — The Psalmist cries from a foreign land for his Lord to rescue him.

Effect on the Psalmist — The Psalmist remembers what his God had promised to him and this acts to refresh him.

How am I unlike the Psalmist — When in severe trouble and when the Lord seems so far from me, I may become despondent and pity myself rather than thanking Him for His eternal love for me.

My response — How often, when in trouble, I am not full of hope and thanks.

My prayer:

You love us wherever we might be,
Your love is not bound by time or space.
We need always to be with You, Lord,
For then we have no worry about place.

The reader's response:

How are you like/unlike with the Psalmist?

____

What is your response to the Psalm?

____

____

What is your prayer?

____

____

Psalm 147

Truth — We could not begin to recount God's grace for His own.

Issues and points — Praise is fitting for our great God. He restores, He gathers, He knows their names, His understanding has no limit, His delight is in all those who hope in His mercy.

Effect on the Psalmist — He can only cry out, "Let God be praised!"

How am I unlike the Psalmist? Although I agree with the cry of the Psalmist, in truth, I confess that my cry is not often enough like his.

My response — Create in me a greater understanding of Your love and grace and cause me to praise You as did the Psalmist.

My prayer:

When I consider all You do for Your own,
Though You are high on heaven's throne,
For You reached down and You did care,
You would not leave your people alone.
And that love that You did show Your own,
Is shown to me, for with You, I am never alone.

The reader's response:

How are you like/unlike the Psalmist?

____

What is your response to the Psalm?

____

____

What is your prayer?

____

____

Chapter 8
When I Cry Out, He Listens

The believer is often under stress, fear, alone, without friends, helpless or anxious. He cries out to his God asking for help and for strength. It is then, when his wonderful, loving, and caring Heavenly Father hears and answers. This truth is very close to that great promise that God loves me (as discussed in Chapter 7).

Psalm 7

Truth — The believer is miserable until he is assured by his God of forgiveness.

Issues and points — The Psalmist has been falsely accused. He turns to his God, Who alone, is able to handle his distress.

Effect on the Psalmist — He seeks refuge in his God, he confesses to Him, and he rejoices in the righteousness of his God.

How am I unlike the Psalmist — How difficult it is for me to leave my burden with the Lord when I have been badly or falsely treated, and then, to be able to rejoice as did the Psalmist.

My response — Lord, it seems that with every Psalm I learn more of my sinfulness and of Your love. Please continue to love me, Lord.

My prayer:

My heart knows the holiness of God,
But it is ever shamed by my sin.
How can I call on You Who are righteous,
When, even as I call, I sin.
How dare I ask You to judge me,
When I am so aware of my sins?
How are You, my righteous God,
Able to accept one like I am?
I do not know, I can only plead,
I do not claim, I can only beg,
I do not deserve, but still I cry,
My God, forgive me, lest I die.

The reader's response:

How are you like/unlike the Psalmist?

____

What is your response to the Psalm?

____

____

What is your prayer?

____

____

Psalm 13

Truth — The Psalmist cries out because it appears that his God has forsaken him.

Issues and points — God is silent and the Psalmist is broken.

Effect on the Psalmist — After crying out, he then trusts and sings to his great God.

How am I unlike the Psalmist — How often I become discouraged when my God appears to be far from me and doesn't answer my prayers.

My response — Lord, teach me and cause me to have peace as does the Psalmist in Your love and mercy.

My prayer:

How often am I alone,
For then You are far from me;
And I think You may have forgotten,
Because I can't hear Your voice.
It is then You assure my heart,
That You, Lord, are there for me.
I may sorrow in my heart,
Not being able to see;
With enemies so strong
I ask, "Will I be able to stand?"
But You, oh Lord, yes, You,
Have comforted and protected me.
It is then I ask myself, how could it be,
That I should ever doubt Your love for me.
Forgive me Lord for ever doubting,
Forgive me for letting fears arise.
I know You are my precious Father,
And here or there, You do care for me.

The reader's response:

How are you like/unlike the Psalmist?

____

What is your response to the Psalm?

____

____

What is your prayer?

____

____

Psalm 22

Truth — The Believer, without his God, is terribly alone.

Issues and points — The Psalmist feels God has left him alone. He cries, he pleads, but he does not sin in his loneliness.

Effect on the Psalmist — The Psalmist continues to trust as he cries out and ends his Psalm with the tremendous response to his prayer, "You do answer!"

How am I unlike the Psalmist? How long do I continue to pray and trust after God has left me alone and does not come to me or comfort me? As I consider the loneliness of the Psalmist and of his faith, I must cry out, "Forgive me Lord for ever doubting Your love."

My response — Father, by Your grace, I will continually trust and rejoice in You.

My prayer:

Lord, You, alone are life,
You, alone, give peace,
You, alone, give hope,
You, alone, give joy.
But I cry and You do not answer,
I am afraid when I am not with You,
Nothing else in life has meaning,
Do answer my humble prayer, today.
Yet, I know You are holy,
For You cannot even look on sin,
And I am sinful in my very heart,
Unless You forgive me, I am undone.

The reader's response:

How are you like/unlike the Psalmist?

____

What is your response to the Psalm?

____

____

What is your prayer?

____

____

Psalm 24

Truth — Our holy, omnipotent God is far above and beyond lowly man.

Issues and points — God is Creator and Sustainer of life, yet He is also holy and righteous. But this great God will receive those who trust in Him for salvation.

Effect on the Psalmist — After acknowledging the majesty and holiness of God, the Psalmist rejoices because this God is his own King of glory.

How am I unlike the Psalmist — He is full of trust and hope in his great God. How often am I not rejoicing in my God and Savior.

My response — Lord, cause me, by Your love and mercy and grace, to also be full of trust and hope in You.

My prayer:

Lord, You have created and sustained all that is,
By what right dare I come to You?
What could I bring or say to You?
I can only come in reverence and fear.
I dare not argue, for You are holy,
I have no rights, You are all-righteous.
I plead only Your mercy and love,
Praying for Your cleansing, by grace.
Accept me, Lord, for Your Name's sake,
Receive me, forgive me, else I die.

The reader's response:

How are you like/unlike the Psalmist?

What is your response to the Psalm?

____

____

What is your prayer?

____

____

Psalm 79

Truth — God, in holiness, requires that we seek His holiness for ourselves.

Issues and points — Man has profaned that which should honor God. God is angry with those who are wicked, but He loves and saves those who trust in Him.

Effect on the Psalmist — He cries out to the God of his salvation and gives thanks to his God.

How am I unlike the Psalmist — When I see the sins of others, does it always draw me closer to my merciful and loving God? Sadly, it doesn't.

My response — Lord, cause me by Your great love, to always consider You in all things and in all events, and to ever praise Your Name.

My prayer:

Lord, when Your anger separates me from You,
The real cause is my own sin.
I freely confess I sin against You,
Forgive me, cleanse me and bring me home.
I repent, I am ashamed, I weep before You,

Until You restore me, I am totally undone,
For You are a God of justice, but praise Your Name,
For You, Lord, are my God of mercy as well.
Thank You for forgiving me, Lord,
Thank You for restoring me to You.

The reader's response:

How are you like/unlike the Psalmist?

____

What is your response to the Psalm?

____

____

What is your prayer?

____

____

Psalm 4

Truth — God listens to the prayers of His own.

Issues and points — God has answered the prayers of the Psalmist in the past. But praying includes repentance and sacrifices to God.

Effect on the Psalmist — He is able to sleep at night for his God keeps him secure.

How am I unlike the Psalmist — Often I am not at rest, as was the Psalmist, and it must be, as with him, because of sin that was not repented of.

My response — Lord, I confess and repent and forsake all my sins. Reveal to me secret or hidden sins that I have not confessed, and not repented of, and not forsaken.

My prayer:

Listen, oh Lord, to me,
Respond to my tearful sorrow,
Give ear unto my prayer,
Attend to my request,
Hear, now, my petition,
Consider my supplication.
You did help me in my need,
Now, once again, be merciful to me.
Let me sleep in peace,
The peace of one brought back to his God.

The reader's response:

How are you like/unlike the Psalmist?

____

What is your response to the Psalm?

____

____

What is your prayer?

____

____

Psalm 5

Truth — The believer knows, by faith, that His God hears him.

Issues and points — The Psalmist prays with sighings and cryings to his great God and Savior. He acknowledges his God is holy, yet merciful, and will protect all who trust in Him.

Effect on the Psalmist — He rejoices that his God will bless him and surround him.

How am I unlike the Psalmist — I do not always pray until I receive God's answer and His blessing.

My response — Lord, cause me to so trust You that I will continue to pray until You do answer.

My prayer:

Lord, hear when I call,
Answer the plea of one poor and needy,
Who cries out to You as he trusts in Your mercy.
Hear my prayer, oh righteous God,
For though You kept me in past distress,
I need Your mercy now.
How long will You forsake me, Lord?
When will You answer me?
Why have You held Your words from me?
Lord, hear me for I trust in You,
Why have You left me so alone?
Lord, I cry out to You unashamed.
Be merciful to me, oh Lord,
Because of Your lovingkindness.
You have answered me,
I praise Your Name;
I cried in repentance and Your heard!
I am now able to sleep in peace,
For You, Lord, do sustain me.

The reader's response:

How are you like/unlike the Psalmist?

____

What is your response to the Psalm?

____

____

What is your prayer?

____

____

Psalm 6

Truth — The Psalmist trusts in and confesses to his God for restoration.

Issues and points — The Psalmist demonstrates how foolish for the believer to *hide* his sins from his God. He admits his weakness, his lack of merit, his sin, his need of forgiveness based on God's love, and his trust in the mercy and love of God.

Effect on the Psalmist — He rejoices that his Lord heard his tears and groanings, his confession, and accepted his prayer.

How am I unlike the Psalmist — I am much like the Psalmist because I delay and do not want to confess my sins. But I am unlike him in that, after He has forgiven me, I am not always as thankful and as full of praise as he was.

My response — Lord, You know how weak, yet stubborn, and sinful I am. Further, You know how slow I am to confess and then to be thankful for Your great grace and mercy. Forgive me, Lord, oh forgive.

My prayer:

Lord, do not rebuke me in Your anger,
Do not discipline me in Your wrath,
Condemn me not in Your indignation.
Be gracious to me for I am so weak,
Forgive me, for I am a great sinner,
Restore me, in love, for I have sinned against You.
I have no merit with You,
I only confess, repent and seek Your mercy.
I only trust in Your grace and love,
Pleading for Your forgiveness.
Lord, do hear and forgive,
Listen and show Your love to me.
Do attend to my pitiful cry,
Do be gracious unto me.
I do not deserve Your love and grace,
But I bow, in trust, before You,
I have no goodness in myself,
Only the goodness You have given to me.
For You, Lord, are most holy,
And You, also are most gracious,
You are ever longsuffering,
So take my sin from me, I pray.

The reader's response:

How are you like/unlike the Psalmist?

____

What is your response to the Psalm?

____

____

What is your prayer?

____

____

Psalm 61

Truth — God answers His own.

Issues and points — The Psalmist tells his God that he is crying out in a loud voice to Him, that his heart is overwhelmed, and that he seeks God's protection under His wings.

Effect on the Psalmist — God has heard and responded.

How am I unlike the Psalmist — Often, I pray, but do not continue until my Lord responds as He did for the Psalmist.

My response — Lord, cause me to continue to plead with You and to call upon You (after having confessed my sins) until You do answer.

My prayer:

How thankful I am that You care for me,
That when I call upon You, You do answer.
Let me always praise Your Name,
For when I call, You do answer.

The reader's response:

How are you like/unlike the Psalmist?

____

What is your response to the Psalm?

____

____

What is your prayer?

____

____

Psalm 64

Truth — We need to cry out to God for help.

Issues and points — The Psalmist tells his God of his laments, and his dangers.

Effect on the Psalmist — He becomes at peace because the Lord has heard and will handle all his troubles.

How am I unlike the Psalmist — How often I am not at peace because of unbelief or lack of trust, which is nothing more than the sin of unbelief.

My response — I am not always at peace from praying, because either I didn't believe God would answer me (sin!) or I hadn't turned my problem entirely over to the Lord (sin!).

My prayer:

Lord, I come because of my trouble,
Yet, I know that You, alone, are holy.
So before I tell You of my sorrows,
Please accept my confession of my sins.
I am unworthy, but You are righteous
I am sinful, but You are holy.

How are You able to receive me,
Why do You take me to Yourself?
I worship You and I reverence You,
And thank You for healing me of pain.

The reader's response:

How are you like/unlike the Psalmist?

____

What is your response to the Psalm?

____

____

What is your prayer?

____

____

Psalm 70

Truth — Our great God is most willing to help His own.

Issues and points — The Psalmist is unafraid to call upon his God for help. He tells his God to hurry!

Effect on the Psalmist — He cries out for all who love God to praise Him.

How am I unlike the Psalmist — Although I may pray for God's help, I do not always think of sharing, with others, how He helped me.

My response — Lord, cause me not only to, in faith, come to You for my needs, but to share your love and response with others.

My prayer:

Deliver me, Lord, for I am in trouble,
And I am poor and needy.
You, Lord, are my only help,
Do make haste to help, oh Lord.
There are many who attack me
And oppose me with evil.
Yet I still rejoice in You alone,
For You do make haste to help me.

The reader's response:

How are you like/unlike the Psalmist?

____

What is your response to the Psalm?

____

____

What is your prayer?

____

____

Psalm 77

Truth — We need to know that our God loves us.

Issues and points — The Psalmist cries out to his God, he seeks Him, he looks to Him, and he knows God's way is holy.

Effect on the Psalmist — He cries, often all night, to his God. He remembers how great was God's response in the past. He realizes that God is holy and that there is no God like his God.

How am I unlike the Psalmist — How often have I cried all night to God? How often have I long meditated on His goodness and love? I confess that it has not been enough.

My response — Forgive Lord, for not trusting You enough, for not believing that You want what is best for me, and most importantly for forgetting that I must worship You and confess my sins to be able to come to You and bring my needs before You.

My prayer:

Give ear for I cry aloud to You, Lord,
I cry out so You may hear me.
In my distress I seek You,
Crying throughout the night.
I cannot sleep,
I often am unable to speak.
I am not yet comforted,
All because of my sin.
But I confess to You, Lord,
Praying that by Your grace, You will forgive.

The reader's response:

How are you like/unlike the Psalmist?

____

What is your response to the Psalm?

____

____

What is your prayer?

____

____

Psalm 80

Truth — We must pray in faith, believing in Him.

Issues and points — The Psalmist calls upon his God, because He is the Shepherd of Israel and the Lord of Hosts.

Effect on the Psalmist — He asks the Lord to cause His people to return and to shine His face upon them.

How am I unlike the Psalmist — I do not pray often enough for all of God's people. I do not have their needs in my thoughts.

My response — Forgive me, again, oh Lord, for failing to love as You love, and for failing to consider all Your children as You do.

My prayer:

Lord, come and restore me,
Cause me to return to You, my loving God.
Shine again upon me,
Then I will be able to praise Your Name to others.
Without You I am lost, Lord,
But my unconfessed sins kept You away,
Now Your grace has driven me to my knees,
Bring me back, bring me back today.
Cause Your face to shine again on me,
Deliver me, again, for Your Name's sake.

The reader's response:

How are you like/unlike the Psalmist?

____

What is your response to the Psalm?

____

____

What is your prayer?

____

____

Psalm 86

Truth — We must come to the Lord, when in trouble.

Issues and points — The Psalmist cries out to God to hear, and answer, and help, and be merciful, and to cause his heart to rejoice.

Effect on the Psalmist — He tells his God He is good, and forgiving, and there is no God like Him.

How am I unlike the Psalmist — How often I forget to thank Him for who He is and for what He has already done.

My response — I need to call upon God to incline His ear to me for I, too, am in distress.

My prayer:

Incline Your ear, oh Lord,
Watch over my soul,
I call out continuously to You,
For You, only, are my God.
I lift my soul to You,
Please hear my prayers,
Please give ear to my pleas,
For I am in deep distress.
Lord, You do answer me,
I praise You with all my heart.

The reader's response:

How are you like/unlike the Psalmist?

____

What is your response to the Psalm?

____

____

What is your prayer?

____

____

Psalm 101

Truth — Lord, when will You come to me?

Issues and points — The Psalmist lists seventeen things he will do for his Lord, asking, then, "When will You come to me?"

Effect on the Psalmist — He is full of faith as he prays and gives promise of his desire to live for his Lord and to worship Him.

How am I unlike the Psalmist — As I consider the long list of burdens he has for serving his Lord, I bow my head and confess my lack of love for my great God and Savior.

My response — Open my heart, Lord, take away all that would keep me from seeing You and worshiping You.

My prayer:

Lord, I sing of Your mercy and justice,
For I desire to follow You.
I do not want to share in any evil,
When, Lord, will You come to me?
I will put away all temptation,
I will reject perversion from my heart,
I will gather Your faithful together,
But when, Lord, will You come to me?

The reader's response:

How are you like/unlike the Psalmist?

____

What is your response to the Psalm?

____

____

What is your prayer?

____

____

Psalm 140

Truth — Unless the Lord saves me, I am undone.

Issues and points-Only the Lord is able to deliver us. For men, without God are violent and wicked.

Effect on the Psalmist — He knows his God is just and will uphold His own in their need.

How am I unlike the Psalmist — I often do not have the peace which comes from casting everything upon Him. I want to help.

My response — Cause me, Lord, to let go and let You take control of my life and provide for all my needs.

My prayer:

I am in great peril, Lord,
And only You can save.
I have no other hope,
You, alone, are God.
Hear my plea for mercy,
Come quickly and rescue me.

The reader's response:

How are you like/unlike the Psalmist?

____

What is your response to the Psalm?

____

____

What is your prayer?

____

____

Psalm 141

Truth — Only God is able to save me.

Issues and points — In asking his Lord to save him, he also asks for clean lips, clean living, and a heart of prayer.

Effect on the Psalmist: He calls on his Lord, and he asks for God to rule in his life.

How am I unlike the Psalmist — I am not as open in my prayer for I do not see the awfulness of my sins as he does.

My response — Lord, cause me to see my sins and to confess them to You and forsake them.

My prayer:

Hasten to help me, give ear to my prayer,
I am undone, Lord, except that You hear.
May my prayer be sweet to You,
May Your answer be quickly, too.

The reader's response:

How are you like/unlike the Psalmist?

____

What is your response to the Psalm?

____

____

What is your prayer?

____

____

Psalm 142

Truth — Only the Lord is able to save.

Issues and points — He cries, he pleads, he pours out his grief, and he tells his Lord all his troubles.

Effect on the Psalmist — He desires to praise the Name of his great God.

How am I unlike the Psalmist — How often do I neglect or forget to give full praise to my great and loving God?

My response — Although I have been in much need, my goal has not always for Him to help do I might praise Him.

My prayer:

I plea to You, my Lord,
I have no other hope.
I pour out my grief,
I tell You all about my woes.
For You do hear me,
And in love, You will answer me.

The reader's response:

How are you like/unlike the Psalmist?

____

What is your response to the Psalm?

____

____

What is your prayer?

____

____

Psalm 143

Truth — God is righteous and answers us in His righteousness.

Issues and Points — God is faithful and righteous. He asks for deliverance as he is becoming weak in spirit and in heart.

Effect on the Psalmist — He has great faith even with his trials and weaknesses.

How am I unlike the Psalmist — He does not seem to be worried, only that his God answer him. I often get emotionally involved when things and situations don't work out.

My response — Cause me, Lord, to trust entirely in You and to lean, totally, upon You.

My prayer:

Hear me and answer my cry,
My soul is weak, my heart stopping.
Answer me quickly, Lord, I pray,
For my very spirit is failing.
I trusted in You,
I need You to show me where to go.
I lift my soul to You,
Asking You to do what I cannot do.
Thank You for Your mercy,
Thank You for rescuing me.

The reader's response:

How are you like/unlike the Psalmist?

____

What is your response to the Psalm?

____

____

What is your prayer?

____

____

Chapter 9
Learning That God Saves Me and Provides for me

Twenty-three Psalms seem to concentrate in these great themes of assurance for the believer. It is almost impossible to read any one Psalm without crying out, "Hallelujah, He saved me!" Perhaps, however, the most important Psalm in this group, is 51 because it provides hope and comfort for every sinning believer.

Psalm 27

Truth — God is our salvation and His Truth gives us light.

Issues and points — Because of our God, we are unafraid. We earnestly want to be with Him. We can cry out loudly to Him, asking for mercy, acceptance, teaching, and protection.

Effect on the Psalmist — He is unafraid, his desire is to be with his Lord, and, to praise Him.

How am I unlike the Psalmist — Such a life-changing Psalm. I confess that my own life is rocky and uneven simply because I do not trust as completely as he does.

My response — Lord, again, I come to you in confession for failing to trust completely and resting and rejoicing in Your mercy.

My prayer:

With God my Light, I do not lose my way,
With Him my Savior, I do not go astray.
Who or what could do harm to me?
How thankful to Him should my life be.
He is worthy of every praise,
My service is only to Him.
For with His choosing me
He caused me, also, to choose Him.
How they relate, He will tell me soon,
Until then, I know Him and He knows me,
These both give my heart certainty.

The reader's response:

How are you like/unlike the Psalmist?

____

What is your response to the Psalm?

____

____

What is your prayer?

____

____

Psalm 107

Truth — God truly satisfies the longing of man's heart.

Issues and points — He is good and His mercy is forever. His watch-care and protecting love for His own is complete and comforting.

Effect on the Psalmist — He cries out, "Give thanks to the Lord for He is good!"

How am I unlike the Psalmist — I know in my head that He is good, but often my heart and life do not show His goodness to others.

My response — Lord, forgive me and continue to teach me Your goodness and mercy until I understand it.

My prayer:

It matters not what I need
Spiritual, physical, or psychological,
Nothing in this life fills my void,
Only You, Lord, can satisfy my heart.
You filled my hungry soul with food,
And took the fear of death away.
You saved me from the oppressor,
Satisfying the longing of my heart.
Send me out, so others may know,
That You satisfy the longing of men's hearts.

The reader's response:

How are you like/unlike the Psalmist?

What is your response to the Psalm?

What is your prayer?

Psalm 69

Truth — Only our God provides redemption through His grace.

Issues and points — The Psalmist is sinking into the watery mire and he cries out to his God. He becomes weary with his tears. But he also know his loving God knows his weaknesses. and will answer him because of His compassion and kindness.

Effect on the Psalmist — He praises his God and commits all those who are harming him to the Lord, and, therefore he does not plan to respond to their evil.

How am I like/unlike the Psalmist — How often have I been in difficulties and, like the Psalmist, cried out to my God and He saved me. But I also have harbored resentment to those who have sought my harm, unlike the Psalmist.

My response — Lord, how often have I been troubled and brought the troubles to You, but kept enmity in my heart. Forgive me, Lord.

My prayer:

Lord, I sink, I cannot stand, I fall,
But You are my redemption.
I weary of my tears, my throat dries out,
But You are my redemption.

I cannot see, I am so foolish,
Even friends go away.
For I bear Your reproach,
But You are my redemption.
I ask for mercy and You hear,
For You, Lord, are my redemption.

The reader's response:

How are you like/unlike the Psalmist?

____

What is your response to the Psalm?

____

____

What is your prayer?

____

____

Psalm 51

Truth — Our loving God causes us to confess to Him.

Issues and points — The Psalmist hid his sin, did not confess, until his God confronted him, then his repentance was genuine and complete.

Effect on the Psalmist — He rejoiced, he confessed, he turned from his sin, he thanked his God, he wanted, again, to be in the center of God's will.

My response — I rejoiced at God's mercy to the unconfessing Psalmist, for, God's love gave me comfort.

My prayer:

Lord, You are holy and yet compassionate,
For You will not let me hide my sin.
Your weight is heavy in my silence,
Unless and until I confess unto You.
How can You, Lord, be so forgiving?
Why do You love me at all?
I now know forgiveness is living,
And silence, terrifying separation from You.
When I confess, I am amazed
For I did sin, yet, You forgave.

The reader's response:

How are you like/unlike the Psalmist?

____

What is your response to the Psalm?

____

____

What is your prayer?

____

____

Psalm 40

Truth — I am helpless without the Lord.

Issues and points — We are in a horrible pit and only our great God can save us. He calls to us and when we respond, how wonderful is His salvation!

Effect on the Psalmist — He has a new song from the Lord for others to hear. He promises to share his God's love and mercy with others.

How am I like/unlike the Psalmist — Yes, I know I have been in a horrible pit and He saved me. But, although He put a new song in my hear, too, how often have I not allowed others to hear it.

My response — Lord, by Your grace, I will tell others of Your salvation and grace.

My prayer:

What can this life really offer?
What could man do to have joy?
For even in a horrible pit,
God placed my feet upon a rock.
Isn't this life, without Him, as a pit,
When God's love is not with me now?
Yes, our life is in a pit or even miry clay
When compared to the joy of God's eternity.
Teach me to always remember, Lord,
That only Your love is forever.

The reader's response:

How are you like/unlike the Psalmist?

What is your response to the Psalm?

What is your prayer?

Psalm 3

Truth — The Lord does truly take care of His won.

Issues and points — The Psalmist is oppressed and attacked by many, but he is able to rest in peace in the security which his great and loving God provides.

Effect on the Psalmist — He is able to say, "I lay down, I slept, I awoke, for the Lord kept me."

How am I unlike the Psalmist — I do not always have the peace of faith as shown by the Psalmist.

My response — Lord, I long for You to cause me to, always have the peace which comes from faith in You.

My prayer:

Lord, I am surrounded,
Men attack me all the day,
Battering me every day.
But I trust entirely in You.

Crying out, in hope, to You,
And You, my Lord, do deliver me.
Now I fall asleep in peace,
For You, Lord, do watch over me.
When awake, there You are upholding me.
Of whom, then, could I be afraid?

The reader's response:

How are you like/unlike the Psalmist?

____

What is your response to the Psalm?

____

____

What is your prayer?

____

____

Psalm 9

Truth — The Psalmist lists some of the great works of his God in taking care of him. He then both praises his God and asks for mercy from Him.

Effect on the Psalmist — He gives thanks, he rejoices, he tells others what his God has done, and he praises his God.

How am I unlike the Psalmist — How often, when surrounded by troubles, I am so busy asking for God's help that I fail to rejoice in what He is doing.

My response — Lord, I am so unthankful for Your love and care — forgive me, please forgive me.

My prayer:

My heart tells me how thankful I should be,
As I consider all that Your do.
You ever protect me and are ever with me,
So nothing harms me, for You are Lord.
And You, my God, reach down to me.
How could I repay this debt,.
How could I be thankful enough?
But, those are not the questions to ask,
But rather, how much love can I give back Thee?

The reader's response:

How are you like/unlike the Psalmist?

____

What is your response to the Psalm?

____

____

What is your prayer?

____

____

Psalm 10

Truth — God is greater than all of those who are against me.

Issues and points — In his trouble, the Psalmist cries out to the Lord "telling" Him that the wicked are everywhere.

Effect on the Psalmist: He rejoices with the words, "You heard the prayer of the lowly, Lord, You establish their heart."

How am I unlike the Psalmist — When troubles arise and the Lord does not seem to be found, it is then I may become dejected. But the Psalmist's faith and his answer from the Lord are wonderful helps for me.

My response — Lord, I confess my lack of faith when in trouble and You do not seem to be answering. Forgive me and come to me, I pray.

My prayer:

When enemies are around me,
When life seems almost gone,
When enemies seek my life at every turn,
And all seems lost, then I turn to You, Lord.
You know, Lord, You do know,
And so nothing will hurt me
Unless You do permit,
For You ever love me and are changing me,
So someday, I will be in Your likeness.
What a day that will be, with sorrow no more,
And I shall see Your face, as Job looked to do.
But only by Your grace and love could that be,
And only because You first did love me.

The reader's response:

How are you like/unlike the Psalmist?

What is your response to the Psalm?

____

____

What is your prayer?

____

____

Psalm 14

Truth — Only by faith in God are we able to prevail.

Issues and points — Many deny even the existence of our God. And unchanged, they spend eternity away and unable to change.

Effect on the Psalmist — He is sorrowful that so many have rejected God.

How am I like the Psalmist — I, too, sorrow over the unbelief of those around me.

My response — Lord, I must try, through Your strength, to win them to You.

My prayer:

How fearful to deny that God is God,
Entering eternity already doomed.
Such is the lot of the godless man,
With no hope, and, too late to change.
To be away from God, forever,
To know, but ever too late.
Still, in this life, does doubt remain,
And death ends nothing, it only begins.

What should I say, whom should I see,
To help take such fear away?
It is not by me, or what I do
Only the love of God makes new.
The reader's response:

How are you like/unlike the Psalmist?

____

What is your response to the Psalm?

____

____

What is your prayer?

____

____

Psalm 31

Truth — No man could stand before a holy God.

Issues and points — God's goodness abounds to those who serve Him. He protects the faithful, but repays those who are proud in full.

Effect on the Psalmist — He hides in the Lord, entrusting his spirit to Him and that is all he needs.

How am I unlike the Psalmist — He praises his God and rests in Him, in the midst of trouble. Often I pray earnestly first and seem to need an answer before I am able to rest.

My response — Teach me, Lord, to trust and rest in You, at the same time.

My prayer:

When I am consumed with grief,
And all my joints are weak,
When I am unable to stand,
I still call on You to save.
I may feel cut off from Your presence,
And can no longer stand,
Then Your arms surround me,
And then You refresh my soul.
Your grace abounds, Your mercy is great,
I thank You for so caring for my soul.

The reader's response:

How are you like/unlike the Psalmist?

____

What is your response to the Psalm?

____

____

What is your prayer?

____

____

Psalm 32

Truth — Our holy God cannot deal with us if we have unconfessed sin.

Issues and points — Unconfessed sin brings God's heavy hand. It results in man's drying up, until he confesses his guilt and forsakes his sin.

Effect on the Psalmist — After confession, he rejoices in God's forgiveness.

How am I like the Psalmist — How often have I failed to confess, and God, in His love, works on me until I confess.

My response — Thank You God for so loving me that You will not let me sin and get away with it.

My prayer:

Lord, I cannot long enjoy sin,
You will not let me, You dry me up.
When I reach to the delights of the world,
Your Holy Spirit does chastise me.
If I do not confess, I become physically sick,
If I continue, I approach death.
Nothing satisfies, nothing will suffice,
Until in my tears, I confess unto You.
You do forgive, You do bring life back to my soul,
And nothing compares with that joy You impart.

The reader's response:

How are you like/unlike the Psalmist?

What is your response to the Psalm?

What is your prayer?

Psalm 35

Truth — God opposes those who would oppose us.

Issues and Insights — The Psalmist cries out for his Lord to fight for him.

Effect on the Psalmist — God answers and the Psalmist exults in his God. He tells us that even his "bones give Him praise."

How am I unlike the Psalmist — He calls out and expects God to help, but I call out and pray for Him to help. The Psalmist exhibited much greater faith than I show.

My response — Lord, forgive me for doubting, but cause me to trust and believe that what you will do, has already been done.

My prayer:

It matters not who may be against me,
Nor how many there may be,
Nor what weapons they have,
For my great God does fight for me.
Who could hope to subdue the Lord?
Who could stand against Him?

My enemies have already lost,
For my God does fight for me.
I have no fears about battle,
Nor do I worry about harm,
They are already defeated,
For my God does fight for me.

The reader's response:

How are you like/unlike the Psalmist?

____

What is your response to the Psalm?

____

____

What is your prayer?

____

____

Psalm 38

Truth — God always loves His own.

Issues and points — The Psalmist has sinned and yet failed to confess. God in love, has brought physical troubles to him, until he cries out, for His God to forgive and heal. The believer cannot *get away* with sin.

Effect on the Psalmist — He finally, totally, trusts in His Lord and confesses to Him.

How am I like the Psalmist — Too often have I sinned and delayed in my prayer of confession and repentance.

My response — Lord, do not let me try to avoid confessing my sins to You, for You are most holy and, in love, You will not tolerate an unconfessed sin in my heart.

My prayer:

Why don't I learn from Your holiness?
Why do I mix my goals with Yours?
Since You have made me Your child,
I cannot hide from Your eye.
Why do I think sin means happiness?
You cannot look at it at all.
But after my sin, You do rein me in,
But my agony sickens my soul.
I repent of my sin, I plea Your cleansing,
Without it I am in misery and pain.
But You are so faithful, You won't let me go,
Why You so love me, I just do not know.

The reader's response:

How are you like/unlike the Psalmist?

____

What is your response to the Psalm?

____

____

What is your prayer?

____

____

Psalm 41

Truth — Lord cause me to confess all of my sins to You.

Issues and points — The Psalmist is desperately ill and he asks his God for healing. He confesses his sins, in his illness, asking for God's mercy.

Effect on the Psalmist — He ends his Psalm with a great note of praise to the Lord God of Israel.

How am I like the Psalmist — I often fail to thank Him in the midst of trials.

My response — Forgive me Lord, for not giving to You, at all times the honor due Your wonderful Name.

My prayer:
Thank You, Lord, for revealing my sins to me,
Thank You for not allowing me to excuse them,
But most of all, thank You, Lord,
For causing me to confess my sins as sins.
How could I expect Your good for me,
If my life has been dirtied by sin?
Sin, caused by my own lust.
But You broke me and loved me,
You are my incomparable God.

The reader's response:

How are you like/unlike the Psalmist?

____

What is your response to the Psalm?

____

____

What is your prayer?

____

____

Psalm 74

Truth — How precious it is to know God and His love for me.

Issues and points — The Psalmist, in pleading cries, calls out to His God to return and help His children. He does not, however, refer to the many sins of the children of Israel when they disobeyed their God.

Effect on the Psalmist — Although he laments God's apparent inaction, he does so, apparently seeking God's mercy and compassion. At the end of the Psalm, he concludes with a prayer of faith in God's mercy.

How am I unlike the Psalmist — He, although God was silent, continued to plead with Him and ask boldly for His compassion. I confess, in fear, that I wonder whether I would have such great faith in such trying situations.

My response — Give me assurance, by Your grace, that You will carry me through bitter times as You did the Psalmist.

My prayer:

I have often been discouraged,
By what godless man has done.
Then I began to covet, and sin,
Until You showed me what You had done.
For I remembered Your deliverance,
In saving the Children of Israel
What an awesome display of grace,
When I considered what You had done.
Lord, I rejoice in Your Name,
For I considered what You have done.

The reader's response:

How are you like/unlike the Psalmist?

____

What is your response to the Psalm?

____

____

What is your prayer?

____

____

Psalm 81

Truth — The sinner, who has not been pardoned carries a huge weight of sin.

Issues and points — When the people cried out to their God in faith, He lifted the burden from their shoulders.

Effect on the Psalmist — He calls out to the people to shout for joy for Who their Lord is and what He has done.

How am I unlike the Psalmist — Although I rejoice that my God has loved me and saved me and protects me, I do not (as the Psalmist did), cry out often enough to the unsaved about our great and merciful God.

My response — Again, my Lord, I confess that I have a silent witness and You want a bold witness. Forgive me.

My prayer:

Thank You, Lord, for rescuing me,
Thank You for offering me Your grace.
I will sing and shout for joy,
For my God lifted my burden from me.
I called, in distress, and You answered.
Because of Your grace, not my sin,
Now I am able to follow You,
For You lifted the burden from me.
I must share Your mercy and love,
For You lifted the burden from me.

The reader's response:

How are you like/unlike the Psalmist?

____

What is your response to the Psalm?

____

____

What is your prayer?

____

____

Psalm 85

Truth — All that our great God provides is good.

Issues and points — God sets the prisoner free, He provides salvation, He gives peace to His people, for He provides the good.

Effect on the Psalmist — He proclaims that lovingkindness, truth, righteousness and peace are provided by his Lord.

How am I unlike the Psalmist — I do not, often enough, rejoice in my great God. It often seems that I must receive something from Him to praise Him.

My response — Cause me, by Your grace, Lord, to love You and praise You, without asking from You.

My prayer:

Lord, You did take away my sin,
Removing it forevermore.
You are not angry with me,
Thank You, Lord, for Your mercy.
Your righteousness gives to us peace,
Your lovingkindness provides us truth.
Our faithfulness to You will increase,
Because You, Lord, did provide the good.

The reader's response:

How are you like/unlike the Psalmist?

____

What is your response to the Psalm?

____

____

What is your prayer?

____

____

Psalm 96

Truth — God, in love, reveals Himself to us.

Issues and points — God has done great things for those that love Him. Someday He will come and judge the earth.

Effect on the Psalmist — He is overwhelmed by the greatness and mercy of his God and Savior.

How am I unlike the Psalmist — As I read the Psalm, it seem clear that the Psalmist is full of hope, faith, and praise for his great God. But as I consider my Lord, I wonder how often I am so full of worship for Him as the Psalmist was.

My response — I confess, Lord, my lack of worship for You.

My prayer:

I sing a new song to You, Lord,
For You made Your Salvation known to me.
I will tell of Your glory and Your work,
For You made Your Salvation known to me.
I will worship You in the beauty of holiness
For You made Your Salvation known to me.
I will be able to come into Your presence,
For You did make Your Salvation known to me.

The reader's response:

How are you like/unlike the Psalmist?

____

What is your response to the Psalm?

____

____

What is your prayer?

____

____

Psalm 102

Truth — The believer's only hope is in the Lord.

Issues and points — The Psalmist is weak, afflicted, lonely and reproached, but he cries out, in faith, to his God for help. His Lord hears and answers him.

Effect on the Psalmist — He has hope and confidence in his God. He is able to praise Him even in trouble.

How am I unlike the Psalmist — He, even when God seems far away, and even when he is in great trouble, is full of hope in his great God, but, too often, my troubles interfere with my worship.

My response — Forgive me, and, cause me to see You and to trust only in You.

My prayer:

Lord, Do not hide Your face from me,
Incline Your ear to hear me,
For I am in great distress,
And I need You to answer my call.
I am becoming as one dead,
I can no longer eat,
I am unclean, outcast by others,
Lord, hear me and set me free.
Thank You for hearing me,
Thank You for making me free.

The reader's response:

How are you like/unlike the Psalmist?

____

What is your response to the Psalm?

____

____

What is your prayer?

Psalm 120

Truth — God cleanses us when we trust in Him.

Issues and points — The Psalmist called out to his God, and God answered him.

Effect on the Psalmist — God answered his prayer.

How am I unlike the Psalmist — I do not pray enough for the Lord to cleanse me of secret and internal sins, unknown to others, but clear to Him.

My response — Lord, I am a sinner and unless You cleanse me and lead me, the old sinful nature will again try to take over.

My prayer:

I called to You in my distress,
You heard, and You answered my prayer.
But You also showed me the sinner I really am,
But You caused me to confess and I was free.
Now I know only You can cleanse me,
And You show me my sin, so You can make me free.

The reader's response:

How are you like/unlike the Psalmist?

What is your response to the Psalm?

____

____

What is your prayer?

____

____

Psalm 124

Truth — Only the Lord is able to help us.

Issues and insights — The believer, without the Lord, is no match for the enemies of God who have been energized by Satan. But God does help and save us.

Effect on the Psalmist — He knows that without the Lord he and all of Israel would have been done in.

How am I unlike the Psalmist — How often have I considered that my strength is sufficient, but God says, His grace is what is sufficient.

My response — Lord, break me, as necessary, to know within my very being that only You and only Your strength matters.

My prayer:

If You were not for me, Lord,
There would be nothing I could do.
For all I could do would be as nothing,
Unless You, Lord, were for me, too.

I praise You, oh, I praise You,
For You love me and You are ever true.
The reader's response:

How are you like/unlike the Psalmist?

____

What is your response to the Psalm?

____

____

What is your prayer?

____

____

Psalm 130

Truth — God, by His grace, forgets the sins of those who trust in Him.

Issues and points — When we cry to God we are already in the deep. We understand that if He remembered our sins we would have no hope.

Effect on the Psalmist — He has trusted in the Lord, and, he hopes in His Word.

How am I like the Psalmist — I, too, have trusted in the Lord, and I, too, hope in His Word. Praise His Name!

My response — Lord, cause me to continually trust in You and hope in Your Word.

My prayer:

How could I stand before You, Lord,
If You had remembered my sin?
I cry from the depths of my heart,
I am unable to keep it in.
But You did forgive me, Lord,
Yes, Lord, You did forgive.
Now I am able to worship You,
For You have forgotten my sin.

The reader's response:

How are you like/unlike the Psalmist?

____

What is your response to the Psalm?

____

____

What is your prayer?

____

____

Psalm 131

Truth — We cannot fellowship with God if we have unconfessed sin.

Issues and points — The Psalmist recognizes that he is able to come to his Lord, only in fearfulness, but in trust.

Effect on the Psalmist — He is humble, thinking only of his Lord, having a quiet and stilled soul, waiting on the Lord.

How am I unlike the Psalmist — When I read this simple, but profound Psalm of purity, prayer, and trust, I realize how far away am I from the holiness displayed here.

My response — Lord, I confess how shabby I really am and how lacking I am in purity and holiness. Forgive me, Lord, do forgive me because of Your grace.

My prayer:

I cannot rest in You, Lord,
With unconfessed sin in my heart,
My soul is not quiet, nor still
Until You do forgive me.

The reader's response:

How are you like/unlike the Psalmist?

____

What is your response to the Psalm?

____

____

What is your prayer?

____

____

Chapter 10
Learning How to Praise the Lord from the Psalmist

Seventeen Psalms seem specifically directed at helping us to learn how to praise our Heavenly Father. Perhaps Psalm 65 is the most startling because it tells us that the believer, before his holy, omnipotent and gracious God, is only able to stand, he is not able, of his own goodness, to offer praise to his God. Therefore, his silence is praise.

Psalm 65

Truth — The silence of the believer before his Lord is praise.

Issues and points — We honor God and worship Him. And He answers our prayers and He forgives our sins, in righteousness.

Effect on the Psalmist — His own sins overwhelm him even as he knows that by faith, his God will atone for them.

How am I unlike the Psalmist — Yes, I know I am a sinner and, yes, I know by faith He will cleanse me, but I haven't yet experienced the soul-wrenching realization that if I am not silent before You I will be adding to my sin.

My response — Lord, I begin, ever so dimly, to catch an understanding of just how holy and pure You are. Forgive me, Lord, for all of my sins, and cause me, to stand before You, in absolute silence.

My prayer:

What right do I have to speak to You,
What good could come from my lips?
You are much higher than I understand,
You are purer than I could ever know.
Even my praise is an affront,
Coming from sinful lips.
But, Lord, I must come, I must plead,
I must praise Your holy Name.
Forgive me and receive me, Lord,
Thank You for Your wonderful grace.

The reader's response:

How are you like/unlike the Psalmist?

____

What is your response to the Psalm?

____

____

What is your prayer?

____

____

Psalm 112

Truth — God, alone, is worthy of our worship.

Issues and points — God blesses those who love Him and He provides light to the upright. They will be firm in their trust of Him, their hearts will be steadfast, and they will not be afraid.

Effect on the Psalmist — He rejoices as he lists all of the blessing of the one who has firmly trusted in his Lord.

How am I unlike the Psalmist — Although I agree with everything the Psalmist has written, yet, by experience I confess that I am not always as joyous and confident as he was.

My response — Lord, cause me, by Your grace, to so realize the joys of trusting in You that nothing could disturb me or set me back.

My prayer:

Lord, You provide completely for me,
You watch over my children,
You lead me when I am in the dark,
You even bless me as I worship You.
You cause me to have compassion,
You keep my heart steadfast,
You remove fear from me,
For You bless me as I worship You.

The reader's response:

How are you like/unlike the Psalmist?

____

What is your response to the Psalm?

____

____

What is your prayer?

____

____

Psalm 117

Truth — God is always worthy of our praise.

Issues and points — We should praise the Lord because His mercy is great and His Truth endures forever.

Effect on the Psalmist — He cries out, in joy, for all the people to praise their great God.

How am I unlike the Psalmist — I confess in being shabby about proclaiming to others of the need and the joy in praising God.

My response — Lord, I confess the sin of not honoring Your holy Name or proclaiming Your righteousness to others.

My prayer:

Lord, You are holy and Truth,
And full of compassion and grace.
Yes, You are ever worthy of praise,
So, just cause me to praise You, Lord.

The reader's response:

How are you like/unlike the Psalmist?

____

What is your response to the Psalm?

____

____

What is your prayer?

____

____

Psalm 132

Truth — The believer must first seek the Lord.

Issues and points — The Psalmist cries out to his God about what he had done for His great God. The Lord answered him with an unbelievable promise that David's descendant will occupy his throne forever.

Effect on the Psalmist — He reports God's answer and promise to him. How amazed he must have been that the great God Whom he served would respond directly and, furthermore, would make such a great promise to him.

How am I unlike the Psalmist — How true, from this Psalm, that David was so in tune with His God that He would both speak to him and promise such a great promise to him. I know that David sinned, but he confessed and repented and was fully restored to his Lord. He was a man after God's own heart, seeing goodness as God saw it, seeing evil, including his own sins as God saw them. Lord, I would be like David in wanting exactly what You want, in my life, in my heart, and in all that I do.

My response — Lord, I thank You for loving me and ask that, as I yield to You, You will draw me ever closer to You.

My prayer:

Lord, teach me, please teach me,
That I must always seek You first.
Then You will provide happiness,
Then You will mightily bless.

The reader's response:

How are you like/unlike the Psalmist?

____

What is your response to the Psalm?

____

____

What is your prayer?

____

____

Psalm 134

Truth — God's people should always praise Him.

Issues and points-God's servants should praise Him. Working for Him does not mean that you are also praising Him. Therefore, whatever we are doing, we still should praise Him.

Effect on the Psalmist — He asks his God to bless those who do praise Him.

How am I unlike the Psalmist — I don't often think of reminding others, and myself, that we all should be praising the Lord. We all get caught up in our needs and wants, rather than praising our great God.

My response — Lord cause me to understand in my heart that praise to You is so good.

My prayer:

Wherever I may be, Lord,
Cause me to praise You.
You are holy and God of creation,
Yet, You have reached down to love me.

The reader's response:

How are you like/unlike the Psalmist?

____

What is your response to the Psalm?

____

____

What is your prayer?

____

____

Psalm 29

Truth — God is in complete charge of the entire universe.

Issues and points — The hosts of heaven are called to honor the Lord, to praise His majesty, and, to worship Him. His voice is above the clouds, and causes all the forces of nature to respond.

Effect on the Psalmist — He sees his God, not only in charge of the universe, but strengthening and blessing His people.

How am I unlike the Psalmist — I have so infrequently seen the majesty and the complete authority of the Lord throughout the universe. I too often think of Him in His relationship to me.

My response — Father, forgive me for limiting You. Forgive me for failing to understand how majestic and omnipotent You are.

My prayer:

Who, Lord, is in this universe of Yours,
Who does not, or will not worship You?
How strange, then, that weak man,
Would dare refuse to bow down?
Those in heaven offer You all they have,
They know Your greatness, they yield in love.
Why then does not man understand?
Why does he challenge Your Name?
Forgive us for being so sinful,
Forgive me for not bringing others to You.
Do cause me to so know Your grace,
That I would share You, as long as I have breath.

The reader's response:

How are you like/unlike the Psalmist?

____

What is your response to the Psalm?

____

____

What is your prayer?

____

____

Psalm 73

Truth — We are able to approach God, when we bow, in reverence, to Him.

Issues and points — The Psalmist often saw and wondered or even coveted what unbelievers had, until he remembered his Holy, loving God.

Effect on the Psalmist — He was jealous and, as a result, was in torment, until he prayed and understood their end.

How am I like the Psalmist — Too often, my envy was like the Psalmist's, but You, in love, caused me, also to know both the end of the ungodly and the joy of the believer with You.

My response — Thank You, Father, for accepting me as I am and for nurturing and helping me to understand Your wonderful love.

My prayer:

Though troubles may surround me,
And I know not what to do,
The future becomes clearer,
When I bow down to You.
You hold me, You guide me,
You wrap Yourself around me.
You cause me to love You,
As I bow down to You.
You receive me in honor
Because I did bow down to You.

The reader's response:

How are you like/unlike the Psalmist?

____

What is your response to the Psalm?

____

____

What is your prayer?

____

____

Psalm 95

Truth — Our great God is most deserving of our praise.

Issues and points — The Psalmist calls for men to sing to their Lord, for He is great, and, He, truly is God.

Effect on the Psalmist — He is overcome by God's holiness and calls for others to come to Him, and not to harden their hearts.

How am I unlike the Psalmist — Although I believe and accept Him, I don't have the evangelical fervor of the Psalmist. That is sin.

My response — Once again, Lord, as I look at the searchlight of Your Word, I have to bow down and confess my sins. Forgive me for not sharing with others about Your love.

My prayer:

Lord, I may come with thanksgiving,
Crying out to You in Psalms,
Making a joyful noise in Your Name
But all I do is so small.
You are great, oh Lord,
You are holy and true.
But what You did in choosing me,
May take eternity for me to understand.
I bow humbly, praying to You,
Confessing my sins, while trusting in You.

The reader's response:

How are you like/unlike the Psalmist?

____

What is your response to the Psalm?

____

____

What is your prayer?

____

____

Psalm 98

Truth — The forgiven believer has a new song in his heart.

Issues and points — God has done wonderful things. He made known His salvation and His righteousness.

Effect on the Psalmist — He cries out for all mankind and even all nature, to shout and praise Him.

How am I unlike the Psalmist — I do not thank Him enough and tell others often enough about His Love.

My response — Lord, every time I read Your Word, it convicts me of selfishness, while telling me of Your love.

My prayer:

You have done so much for me, Lord,
You made known Your salvation to me,
You showed me Your righteousness,
And, now, I sing a new song to You.
You showed me Your mercy,
You remembered me, by grace,
Yet, Lord, I am so unworthy,
For not bringing others to Your Holy Place.

The reader's response:

How are you like/unlike the Psalmist?

____

What is your response to the Psalm?

____

____

What is your prayer?

____

____

Psalm 105

Truth — Our God is most worthy for Who He is and what He does.

Issues and points — The Psalmist praises God for His Name, and His wonderful works. He recites many of the miracles and examples of God's love in the past, asking men to give glory to His Holy Name.

Effect on the Psalmist — He is full of rejoicing and evangelism, asking men to give glory to the very Name of God.

How am I unlike the Psalmist — I do not ask often enough for others to give glory to the very Name of our holy God.

My response — Lord I confess to being selfish with Your love.

My prayer:

Lord, You are gracious and You are kind,
Protecting me in distress and in hurt.
Now I need to share Your goodness,
Now I need to sing Your greatness.
To tell of Your wonderful works,
To give glory to Your Name,
So others could rejoice in their hearts,
And become Your children as I am.
The reader's response:

How are you like/unlike the Psalmist?

____

What is your response to the Psalm?

____

____

What is your prayer?

____

____

Psalm 121

Truth — Only by looking to the Lord do we know the Truth.

Issues and points — The Psalmist tells us his help is from the Lord, and He made all things. In addition, He keeps us, and He protects us.

Effect on the Psalmist — He is at perfect peace because His God is in charge and cares for him.

How am I unlike the Psalmist — The peace which is evident in the Psalm is not always a description of me. Many times, by taking my eyes off the Lord, or by failing to read His Word or trust Him totally, I do not have that peace.

My response — Once again, Lord, I confess that my eyes are not on You and then I get into all kinds of difficulties. Forgive me and restore me, I pray.

My prayer:

Lord, in times past, You spoke from the mountain,
Now I look for You to speak to me.
You keep me and shelter me,
You do always protect me.
I know that, Lord, I really do,
But increase my faith and trust in You.

The reader's response:

How are you like/unlike the Psalmist?

____

What is your response to the Psalm?

____

____

What is your prayer?

____

____

Psalm 122

Truth — Worshiping God is both a privilege and blessing.

Issues and points — The Psalmist tells of many who go to worship their great God. He calls on them to pray for Jerusalem and the house of God.

Effect on the Psalmist — He rejoices when going to the house of the Lord.
How am I unlike the Psalmist — Lord, it often seems that part of my going to Your house is from duty, not for worship, alone. Forgive me, Lord.

My response — Lord, may I never lose the excitement and the anticipation of going to Your house to worship You.

My prayer:

What a wonderful privilege to have,
Being able to worship You, Lord.
You, Who are mighty and holy,
You, in grace, allow me to speak to You.
I have nothing in myself,
And nothing to give to You,
Except my heart, Lord, except my heart.

The reader's response:

How are you like/unlike the Psalmist?

____

What is your response to the Psalm?

____

____

What is your prayer?

Psalm 135

Truth — God is ever worthy of praise.

Issues and points — The Psalmist calls for all to praise God for He, only, is God, He is caring, gracious, and giving, and He is merciful to His servants.

Effect on the Psalmist — He is overflowing with praise for his great God.

How am I unlike the Psalmist — Although I trust in Him and I seek, always to do His will, I confess that the rejoicing on the part of the Psalmist is not a 24 hour a day experience for me.

My response — Lord I confess that I do not rejoice in You and Your care as I should. Forgive me and change me.

My prayer:

Lord, Your Name is great, You rule over all
Yet You did choose me, and I am but nothing.
You redeemed me, You took me to Yourself,
You are ever in charge, Lord.
But I must be willing to do all You ask,
And by Your grace, I will, Lord, I will.

The reader's response:

How are you like/unlike the Psalmist?

____

What is your response to the Psalm?

____

____

What is your prayer?

____

____

Psalm 146

Truth — Our great God is ever worthy of our praise.

Issues and points — The Psalmist asks that he praise his God throughout his entire life. He tells us that happy is the man who is helped by the Lord.

Effect on the Psalmist — He is constantly praising his God.

How am I unlike the Psalmist — How often do I allow things, or the pressures of this life or even duties to cause me to forget to be constantly praising my God in my heart.

My response — Lord, again, as I read Your divine Word, You show me about another part of my life that needs to turned over to You. I ask You to cause me to have praise for You on my heart and lips all the day.

My prayer:

Lord, You are ever worthy,
I could never praise You enough.
You are Creator and Sustainer,
And for me, Lord, You are Savior as well.

The reader's response:

How are you like/unlike the Psalmist?

____

What is your response to the Psalm?

____

____

What is your prayer?

____

____

Psalm 148

Truth — The Lord, alone, is ever worthy of praise.

Issues and points — Wherever we are, the Lord is to be praised. Everyone and everything is called upon to praise Him.

Effect on the Psalmist — He is overcome by the greatness and worthiness of his God.

How am I unlike the Psalmist — I confess that the recognition that all life and all that was created is to praise Him, has not often been part of my consciousness. But He is Lord and He is worthy of all praise.

My response — Forgive me, Lord, and cause me to seek, ever both to praise You and call on all to praise You as well.

My prayer:

Whether in heaven above or earth below,
Let everyone and everything praise the Lord.
Whether angels or creatures here below,
Let everyone praise the Lord.
For though You have all power,
You have loved even me.
I joyously join the refrain,
Praise be to the Lord.

The reader's response:

How are you like/unlike the Psalmist?

____

What is your response to the Psalm?

____

____

What is your prayer?

____

____

Psalm 149

Truth — God, our Savior is worthy of a new song.

Issues and points — The Psalmist calls for a new song to his Lord, in the assembly. Let His people rejoice and shout for joy, even when they are alone.
Effect on the Psalmist — He is constantly rejoicing.

How am I unlike the Psalmist — I am not constantly rejoicing in my great God.

My response — Forgive me and do cause me, by Your grace, to be constantly rejoicing in You.

My prayer:

Lord, You created and You sustain all things,
And, yet, You allowed me to be with You.
I don't understand Your grace,
But, with joy, I receive my new life from You.

The reader's response:

How are you like/unlike the Psalmist?

____

What is your response to the Psalm?

____

____

What is your prayer?

____

____

Psalm 150

Truth — God allows us to praise Him by music.

Issues and points — All instruments may praise Him.

Effect on the Psalmist — He says the music must be from the heart.

How am I unlike the Psalmist — I don't always recognize this truth.

My response — Forgive me, Lord.

My prayer:

Whatever instrument is used for praise,
It is to glorify Your Name.
And such music unites heart and soul,
If worship is always its aim.

The reader's response:

How are you like/unlike the Psalmist?

____

What is your response to the Psalm?

____

____

What is your prayer?

____

____

Chapter 11
Learning to Hide Myself in Him

There are seven Psalms which bring the comfort and assurance of our knowing we are able hide in the Lord, under His wings, where He is and hiding in His secret place.

Psalm 46

Truth — The Psalmist gives us the amazing truth that we are able to find refuge, or, hide in the Lord.

Issues and points — God is always near in our distress. He is all-powerful and there is nothing or no one that could move us from our Lord.

Effect on the Psalmist — He does not fear for his God is his refuge and his strength.

How am I unlike the Psalmist — I do not always have the assurance of the Psalmist and it is because I have not confessed some sin and committed it to Him.

My response — Lord I confess that I harbor secret sins and don't confess them. It is then that I am helpless.

My prayer:

Lord, You are my haven of refuge,

I can rest, without fear, in You.
You are always near, in my time of need,
For You do watch over me at all times.
I have confidence in You, Lord,
For You made me safe in Your love,
You gave me peace by Your grace,
And all my joy comes from You.

The reader's response:

How are you like/unlike the Psalmist?

____

What is your response to the Psalm?

____

____

What is your prayer?

____

____

Psalm 57

Truth — God always protects His own.

Issues and points — The Psalmist seeks refuge under His wings, and, he called out to his God, knowing God would help him.

Effect on the Psalmist — He is confident in his Lord and sings praise unto Him.

How am I unlike the Psalmist — I do not always rejoice in what He does or has for me.

My response — Cause me, Lord, by Your grace to ever be rejoicing in You.

My prayer:

What protection I receive from the Lord,
For I hide under the shadow of His wings.
It matters not what troubles arise
For I hide under the shadow of His wings.
Men attack, wherever I am,
But such troubles do not avail,
And I fear not, where I am,
For I am hiding under His wings.
I will share my Lord with those I meet,
For I am hiding under His wings.

The reader's response:

How are you like/unlike the Psalmist?

____

What is your response to the Psalm?

____

____

What is your prayer?

____

____

Psalm 59

Truth — The Lord always receives His own.

Issues and points — The Psalmist asks his God to deliver him. He describes them as bloodthirsty, always thinking they are safe.

Effect on the Psalmist — He knows his God, in mercy, will come, that He is his shield, and he is able to rejoice at what his God does for him.

How am I unlike the Psalmist — Though I trust Him, I often want to take matters into my own hand. How can He be triumphant when I am trying to do it myself?

My response — Lord teach me to lean totally upon You and to rejoice in what You do for me.

My prayer:

Lord, when I cry to You for mercy,
When I plead for deliverance,
I have peace because I know
You are my Hiding Place.
When I fear what may befall me,
When I look at those against me,
I have peace because I know
You are my Hiding Place.
Thank You, Lord, for Your love and grace,
Thank You for being my Hiding Place.

The reader's response:

How are you like/unlike the Psalmist?

What is your response to the Psalm?

____

____

What is your prayer?

____

____

Psalm 71

Truth — Our gracious Lord has determined to save us.

Issues and points — God is righteous, He is my Rock, my Confidence, my Assurance, my God and my Lord.

Effect on the Psalmist — He praises Him, and tells of His goodness and salvation.

How am I unlike the Psalmist — He cries out about his Lord, but I am often taken up by the affairs of this life and forget or neglect to do so.

My response — Forgive me, Lord, for not making You the center of my life at all times.

My prayer:

Lord, You took my reproach away,
And set me free.
You are my confidence and trust,
And I hide myself in You.
You bend down and You listen,
And You save without delay.
For You, are my Deliverer,
And I hide myself in You.

The reader's response:

How are you like/unlike the Psalmist?

____

What is your response to the Psalm?

____

____

What is your prayer?

____

____

Psalm 84

Truth — To be with the Lord is precious.

Issues and points — The Lord's dwelling-place is precious. Happy is everyone who dwells with Him.

Effect on the Psalmist — He shouts to his God. He looks to Him as his shield. He looks forward to spending eternity in His courts.

How am I unlike the Psalmist — He is consumed with his great God and I find myself, often, thinking abut the matters of this life, instead.

My response — Again, Lord, as I read Your Word, I am convicted for not loving You enough and not having faith enough. Cause me to desire Your will only.

My prayer:

I long to be with You, Lord,
For where You are is precious.
And as a bird rests in its nest,
So I rest when I am with You, Lord.
While on this earth, may You stay with me,
Cause me to confess and be clean,
To retain fellowship with You,
For where You are is precious.

The reader's response:

How are you like/unlike the Psalmist?

____

What is your response to the Psalm?

____

____

What is your prayer?

____

____

Psalm 90

Truth — The believer is always at home with the Lord.

Issues and points — God has been his people's dwelling place for generations. Only the Lord is God.

Effect on the Psalmist — He cries out for God's mercy and trusts in his grace.

How am I unlike the Psalmist — He continued to cry out to his God even when He appeared not to answer. I have not been in such a silent time and rejoice in that, but pray that whatever comes, I will be faithful to Him as was the Psalmist.

My response — Lord, continue to hold me up, to strengthen me, and to give me Your faith.

My prayer:

Lord, my life only has meaning in You,
But how often do I grieve You with sin?
How could I offend in so many ways,
Forgive me, Lord, for I have sinned.
Life on this earth is but a breath,
To begin and pass almost at once.
Take me into eternity with You, Lord,
Cause me to trust wholly in You.
I love You, my Lord,
And I rest wholly in You.

The reader's response:

How are you like/unlike the Psalmist?

____

What is your response to the Psalm?

____

____

What is your prayer?

____

____

Psalm 91

Truth — To be with the Lord is most precious.

Issues and points — In God's secret place we are kept from attacks of all kinds, and we always be delivered by Him.

Effect on the Psalmist — He has complete confidence under His wings.

How am I unlike the Psalmist — I do not often enough *see* that I am under His wings and therefore I do not rejoice as he does.

My response — Cause me, Lord, by Your great mercy and grace, to cause me to see, at all times, that I am under the shadow of Your wings.

My prayer:

Lord, I want to abide in Your shadow,
I want You to be my refuge.
For You are my God and Savior,
And I trust wholly in You.
You deliver me for You love me,
You lift me because I know Your Name,
You always rescue me when in trouble,
You do answer me, when I do call.

The reader's response:

How are you like/unlike the Psalmist?

____

What is your response to the Psalm?

____

____

What is your prayer?

____

____

Chapter 12
Learning to Serve the Lord and Tell Others about Him

There are eighteen Psalms which describe what I should be doing for my Lord in view of all He has done for me. Psalm 53 begins with the important prayer of the Psalmist that he love others. The others deal with serving God because He has asked us to (82), hating evil (97), giving back to God (116), sharing God's love with tears for those we meet (126), admitting that any work really is God's work (127) and twelve others (1,15,17,18, 50, 52, 78,115, 125,128, 133, and 138) on serving our great God.

Psalm 53

Truth — God loves all men and women and desires that they trust in Him.

Issues and points — Foolish men deny that God exists.

However, when God looks upon all men, "no one was righteous", the Psalmist tells us.

Effect on the Psalmist — The Psalmist is in wonderment that all men are unrighteous, and he worries about their future.

How am I unlike the Psalmist — The Word of God has clearly said over and over that all are sinners and all (including me) have not met the righteous requirement of a holy God. My response is that, without God's love and grace, I, too, am unrighteous and unfit to be drawn into the Father's kingdom.

My response — Father, inasmuch as You in grace and mercy, saved me, and You would have all men to be saved, I must love those with whom I meet so that I can share Your love with them.

My prayer:

When I consider that God has loved me,
Although within me was nothing worthy,
Why then should I not love others,
All sinners just like me?
That You do love sinners is proved
My own life is evidence enough.
Why, then, am I unwilling,
To share Your love to others who are lost?
Forgive me Lord, cause me to change
So I, too, may share Your great love.

The reader's response:

How are you like/unlike the Psalmist?

____

What is your response to the Psalm?

____

____

What is your prayer?

____

____

Psalm 82

Truth — God wants believers to tell others of His love and grace.

Issues and points — The Psalmist states that God holds His leaders accountable for showing His love and telling others about His love.

Effect on the Psalmist — The Psalmist gives us what God has said about unfaithful religious leaders. Without any personal comments by the Psalmist, I believe the Psalmist agreed with his God, and therefore, was saddened over the sins of such men.

How am I like the Psalmist — The Psalmist tells us of the sins of leaders in not bringing men to the Lord. I, too, am saddened when such leaders continue to *teach* the Word. I, like the Psalmist, (I believe) must share God's love and grace, whether or not others do so.

My response — Lord, cause me to faithfully represent You.

My prayer:

Lord, I think of Your righteous judgments,
Of Your care for the oppressed.
But now I must represent You to others,
So Your goodness and mercy, may be known.
In myself, Lord, I cannot do this,
But I remember how You helped me,
And I will show that to those I meet,
Because You asked me to represent You.
Each day I confess my unworthiness,
But You did ask me to represent You.

The reader's response:

How are you like/unlike the Psalmist?

What is your response to the Psalm?

____

____

What is your prayer?

____

____

Psalm 97

Truth — Our holy God cannot look upon evil.

Issues and Points — God is Lord of all, and all shall bow down to Him. Those who love Him are admonished to hate evil, also.

Effect on the Psalmist — He sings praises to the Name of his God.

How am I unlike the Psalmist — The majestic vision of the Psalmist with respect to God's kingdom and His activities are amazing to me. How, in faith, he was able and permitted to see this is beyond me. Certainly, he was a precious child of the King. I, too, am precious to my Lord, but I haven't been, and I don't expect to be blessed in this manner.

My response — Thank You, Lord, for loving me. Whatever You have in store for me is, I know, perfect, because You are both loving and perfect.

My prayer:

Lord, You are holy and You hate evil,
But You love me.
You brought me to You in love,
Why then, Lord, don't I hate evil also?

I repent, I confess, I bow down to You,
I plead Your mercy and abhor my sin.
For You are holy and You do hate evil,
Why, then, do I not hate evil as well?
Cause me to be so broken by Your love,
That I, too, will hate evil also.

The reader's response:

How are you like/unlike the Psalmist?

____

What is your response to the Psalm?

____

____

What is your prayer?

____

____

Psalm 116

Truth — God listens to and hears those who love Him.

Issues and points — The Lord inclines His ear to His own. He is gracious, righteous, and full of compassion. A believer's death is precious to the Lord, perhaps, because now that one is ever with the Lord.

Effect on the Psalmist — He writes, "I love the Lord for He heard my cry from my heart."

How am I unlike the Psalmist — His joy and his trust are so much greater than mine that I have to confess to the Lord, the shabbiness of my faith.

My response — Forgive me, Lord, for not committing my all to You.

My prayer:

Lord, You hear my heart's cry,
You bend Your ear and listen to me,
You wash my tears away,
What could I give back to You?
You have compassion for me,
Even my death would be precious to You,
For, then You would bring me to Yourself.
What could I give back to You?
Lord, as You give me breath and strength,
Allow me to always praise Your Name.

The reader's response:

How are you like/unlike the Psalmist?

____

What is your response to the Psalm?

____

____

What is your prayer?

____

____

Psalm 126

Truth — Telling others of God's love requires our tears.

Issues and points — We rejoice in the Lord, but we weep, as we share His love with others.

Effect on the Psalmist — He loved his Lord, but, he, too, wept as he told others about his Lord.

How am I like the Psalmist — When I present God's love to an unsaved person, I find myself weeping for his soul.

My response — Lord, continue to allow me to share Your goodness.

My prayer:

Bringing someone to trust in You,
Required a sacrifice, first, from You.
But all it takes from my yielded heart,
Is Your love shining through my tears.
If You could rescue me from sin,
And, if You want others too,
Why can't I give my yielded heart,
In tears, to work for You?
For then the sinner accepts Your mercy,
And he, by Your grace, and Your mercy, is free.

The reader's response:

How are you like/unlike the Psalmist?

____

What is your response to the Psalm?

____

____

What is your prayer?

Psalm 127

Truth — God does His work, but, in grace, He allows us to help.

Issues and points — Unless God saves, man's work is in vain. But that He does save, He also allows us to share in this great work.

Effect on the Psalmist — He trusts totally in his Lord and he knows that unless the Lord is in charge, all of his labors are for nothing.

How am I unlike the Psalmist — Too often, in my enthusiasm to share Christ, I go before Him and then it becomes my work alone, which is vain.

My response — Lord, cause me to ever be sensitive to Your leading and direction. Never allow me to presume to bring people to You, by myself.

My prayer:

You must do the work, Lord,
You must do the work.
Yet we must also work, too,
But ever depending upon You.
There is nothing alone which we could do,
We must always depend upon You.
For You must do the work, Lord,
Then, by Your grace, You let us help, too.

The reader's response:

How are you like/unlike the Psalmist?

____

What is your response to the Psalm?

____

____

What is your prayer?

____

____

Psalm 15

Truth — The Lord is the One we serve and love.

Issues and points — Unless we live as You would have us live, we could not live with You. Yet, only by Your grace are we able to do that.

Effect on the Psalmist — He trusts in his Lord to keep him thinking and acting righteously.

How am I like the Psalmist — I, too, depend on my Lord to make me and keep me righteous by His grace.

My response — Lord, only by Your grace am I able to come to You. Only by the faith You gave to me am I able to trust in You.

My prayer:

What must I do to live with You,
Though all I might do would not be enough.
For You require holiness, kindness, truth,
Purity and reverence for You.
Oh Lord, of myself I cannot be as You are,
For sin exists within me.
But I can trust in Your grace,
That You will make me what I should be.
I worship You, I come to You,
Thank Your, Lord, for accepting me.

The reader's response:

How are you like/unlike the Psalmist?

____

What is your response to the Psalm?

____

____

What is your prayer?

____

____

Psalm 1

Truth — God's Word gives blessing to those who trust in Him.

Issues and points — The one who avoids those who hate God is blessed. For wicked men will suffer for eternity, except they repent, confess and trust in God.

Effect on the Psalmist — He is at peace, with his God, as he tells us these truths.

How am I like/unlike the Psalmist — I agree with the Psalmist, but he has been uniquely blessed of God to be permitted to pen these great truths.

My response — Thank You, Lord, for loving me.

My prayer:

Lord, as I read Your Word
I delight in Your teaching.
I, too, need to study it day and night,
For I am frail, and do go astray.
How I need Your guidance and blessing
Unless You lead I fall away.
Thank You, Lord, for watching over me.
I am safe while staying in Your care.
Establish me through Your Word,
Then use me, Lord, I pray, for You.

The reader's response:

How are you like/unlike the Psalmist?

____

What is your response to the Psalm?

____

____

What is your prayer?

____

____

Psalm 17

Truth — What God desires of us is our most important goal of all.

Issues and points — We have to cry out to our Lord because of Who He is and because of our great need. We have to trust in His goodness and that He will answer us.

Effect on the Psalmist — He knows his God will answer. He wants only to do and be what his God has planned for him.

How am I unlike the Psalmist — He writes in perfect peace, being so close to his Lord. My prayer and my desire is that I, too, might be that close with my Savior and Lord.

My response — Lord, I want to be totally in Your will.

My prayer:

Lord, You are righteous, I call only to You,
But what should I ask of You, I pray?
For You, alone, are holy and pure
While I am mere man, a sinner, of clay.
But You gave me Your life and Your love,
So that even when I stray away,
You, lovingly, forgive, as soon as I ask,
And by Your grace, You took my sin away.
So, I call again to You,
What should I ask of You, I pray?
I want to be pure, like You, I do not want to sin,

I want clean thoughts and Your love within.
If I may worship You, then I can rejoice,
For You have accepted my plea.
You, my Savior, took my sin away.
Then I can be Your voice, to those who ask.

The reader's response:

How are you like/unlike the Psalmist?

____

What is your response to the Psalm?

____

____

What is your prayer?

____

____

Psalm 18

Truth — God is ever worthy of our love.

Issues and points — The Psalmist calls his God by many Names: Lord, my Strength, my Rock, my Shield, the Horn of my Salvation, my High Tower, the Highest, and my Deliverer.

Effect on the Psalmist — He can only cry out, "I love You, Oh Lord."

How am I unlike the Psalmist — His rejoicing and his outburst of praise shames me, not because of jealousy, but because I see my own life far less aware of my great God and failing to rejoice in Him.

My response — Lord, in humility, I cry out to You to forgive me and to bless me with the joy of the Psalmist.

My prayer:

How could I ever show my love to You, Lord,
For You have done so much for me.
You hold me, protect me, and deliver me,
You save me from all my enemies.
I cry out for Your answer,
Death threatens and You do rescue,
You constantly take me away from trouble,
You bring me to where You are.
And though I sin, causing You hurt,
In love and grace, You forgive.
I do not understand why You do love me,
But I thank You, oh yes, I thank You.

The reader's response:

How are you like/unlike the Psalmist?

____

What is your response to the Psalm?

____

____

What is your prayer?

____

____

Psalm 50

Truth — All that is good, we have from our great God.

Issues and points — God speaks, telling the people that He doesn't need them, but they, in their sins, desperately need Him. God is offended when they insincerely quote His laws and do not believe them or follow them.

Effect on the Psalmist — He acts as God's servant in the giving of this most solemn message.

How am I unlike the Psalmist — The Psalmist was chosen by His God to deliver this message. I rejoice that his God found him worthy, though I am not. And as I read the list of those things which were offensive to my holy God, I confess that many apply to me.

My response — Forgive me Lord for continuing to be an unclean servant.

My prayer:

Lord, You are Almighty, there is none but You,
You sit in righteousness and in judgment.
But what do You want from me
What can I offer to You?
You do not need burnt offerings,
You want my heart.
Only then when I call on You,
Will You both hear and answer.
How simple, but how difficult,
Yet, to yield, to only need to love You.

The reader's response:

How are you like/unlike the Psalmist?

____

What is your response to the Psalm?

____

____

What is your prayer?

____

____

Psalm 52

Truth — God loves all men and desires that all men trust Him.

Issues and points — Those who oppose God are permitted to do so only by His great mercy.

Effect on the Psalmist — He trusts totally in God's mercy and thanks Him what He has done.

How am I unlike the Psalmist — He forth-tells God's Word but is still, by God's grace able to rest in His love. I am not as close to the Lord as he is.

My response — Forgive me, Lord, and draw me closer to You.

My prayer:

Lord, You create and You do sustain,
All men will submit to You.

But I thank You that You did call me,
And I was allowed to respond to Your plea.
In this life some will reject You,
By doing so, they are lost.
Still, I must share Your grace and love,
That others might receive You, too.
The reader's response:

How are you like/unlike the Psalmist?

____

What is your response to the Psalm?

____

____

What is your prayer?

____

____

Psalm 78

Truth — The believer should tell others of God's love.

Issues and points — The Psalmist records how God took can of the children of Israel even though they often sinned against Him. God was always in charge, but sinful men would not accept Him or obey Him.

Effect on the Psalmist — He is concerned for his own people and he wants to tell them again of how great God is and what He has done and is doing.

How am I unlike the Psalmist — It seems clear that God's message is being carried forth by one who loves both his great God and his own sinful people. He doesn't give up his message because he still loves his people. I confess my love does not seem to be as compassionate nor as constant.

My response — Make me, Lord, make me to totally love You, yet to love my people as well.

My prayer:

Let me not be silent about You, oh Lord,
Let me not be silent.
You are loving, and compassionate,
You are strong, yet with mercy.
Without Your mercy, I would be dust
Without Your mercy I would fall,
Without Your mercy I would not be with You,
Without Your mercy, I could not live at all.
Lord, do cause me to tell of Your greatness,
For You have been so gracious to me.

The reader's response:

How are you like/unlike the Psalmist?

____

What is your response to the Psalm?

____

____

What is your prayer?

____

____

Psalm 115

Truth — Men continue to reject their sovereign God.

Issues and points — Glory is due the Name of God. He is our Helper and Defender, even though He is also Creator.

Effect on the Psalmist — He calls on his people to trust in the Lord.

How am I unlike the Psalmist — In his worship, he turns to his people and encourage them as well. I need to have this love for my kinsmen and brethren as he does.

My prayer — Lord, in Your grace, expand my vision to include those You have given to me. Cause me, always, to love and serve them as well.

The reader's response:

How are you like/unlike the Psalmist?

____

What is your response to the Psalm?

____

____

What is your prayer?

Psalm 125

Truth — The Lord keeps and saves those who trust in Him.

Issues and points — Faithful believers are compared to Mount Zion, which does not move.

Effect on the Psalmist — He calls for his Lord to show Himself to be good to all those that are upright in heart.

How am I unlike the Psalmist — Once again, his love is so expansive, whereas often mine is circumscribed by my family and my church.

My response — Lord, again I must call on You to open my vision to see all those that love You.

My prayer:

Lord, You are my defense and my strength,
And there is nothing You cannot stay.
No other power in the universe is able to move You,
Except my faith in Your Name.
And even then, You did draw me,
For I had no worth of my own,
But that which you placed in me,
And, thus, I will never be alone.

The reader's response:

How are you like/unlike the Psalmist?

\

What is your response to the Psalm?

What is your prayer?

Psalm 128

Truth — God is ever deserving of our reverence.

Issues and points — Those who fear the Lord are blessed. Their families are kept by Him.

Effect on the Psalmist — He is both happy and at peace.

How am I unlike the Psalmist — Lord, as I read of the promises to the man who fears the Lord, I cry out, forgive me, Lord, and take care of my family as the Psalmist promises.

My response — Again, Lord, I commit my family, by faith, to Your care.

My prayer:

Lord, You must have my total surrender,
Nothing less will do.

I cannot claim Your help,
When I haven't surrendered all to You.
Lord, I do submit all to You,
But, I also claim the promises in this Psalm,
I commit all of my family in faith,
For I believe You will answer my call.

The reader's response:

How are you like/unlike the Psalmist?

____

What is your response to the Psalm?

____

____

What is your prayer?

____

____

Psalm 133

Truth — We are able, only by God's grace, to love each other.

Issues and points — The love of family and brothers and sisters in the Lord, is precious. And it is given to us by our wonderful Lord.

Effect on the Psalmist — He tells us love for family and other believers is both pleasant and good.

How am I unlike the Psalmist — I have not yet had the wonderful and precious love for all the family of God as does the Psalmist.

My response — Never let me forget, Lord, that all of your children are in my family, too.

My prayer:

How good for brothers to dwell in unity,
Brought together in peace and harmony.
But only You can cause that to take place, Lord,
And then only when we completely love You.
If we so love You, Lord,
Love for others will soon follow.

The reader's response:

How are you like/unlike the Psalmist?

____

What is your response to the Psalm?

____

____

What is your prayer?

____

____

Psalm 138

Truth — We must thank God with our whole heart for what He has done for us.

Issues and points — The Psalmist gives thanks to God with his whole heart, and before all others. He praises God's Name for His mercy and truth and for His answers to the Psalmist's prayers.

Effect on the Psalmist — He thanks God, he sings to Him, he bows before Him and he praises the Name of God.

How am I unlike the Psalmist — When I see the completeness with which the Psalmist loved his God, I am ashamed.

My response — Lord, You are so good and holy, yet You have loved me. Cause me, by Your grace, to show my love and thanks to You.

My prayer:

You have lifted up Your Name, Lord,
You have magnified Your Truth.
And, then, You showed me Your mercy,
When You did care for me.
What could I give to You, Lord,
For all that You have given me?

The reader's response:

How are you like/unlike the Psalmist?

____

What is your response to the Psalm?

____

____

What is your prayer?

____

____

Chapter 13
I Want to Spend Eternity with My Lord

God's plan for us is to bring us unto Himself for all eternity.

Now, as believers we also want to be with Him. Five Psalms address this subject, but Psalm 88 approaches the subject with, it seems, just a little humor.

Psalm 16

Truth — Only the Lord is able to satisfy the Heart.

Issues and points — The Psalmist begins by asking for God's watch-care in this life, but ends by rejoicing that his God will take him to be with Him eternally.

Effect on the Psalmist — He is at perfect peace, while here and in considering the future with his Lord.

How am I unlike the Psalmist — He was at perfect peace after he asked his Lord for that peace in the middle of trouble. I, too, need to have that perfect peace as he did.

My response — Lord, just as the Psalmist asked for Your peace, I, too, ask for Your peace. The Psalm records that he, in fact, did receive Your perfect peace.

My prayer:

This life is but a vapor, soon to be no more,
Yet man, in his heart, desires more.
But only through trusting in the God of grace,
Could any experience joy forevermore.
I thank the Lord, my God,
And I love Him for Who He is,
But I also praise Him for promising to me,
That I will be with Him for eternity.
How, then, could I not tell of my God,
How could I ever not serve Him?
For He, in love, has promised me,
I will have joy with Him for all eternity.

The reader's response:

How are you like/unlike the Psalmist?

____

What is your response to the Psalm?

____

____

What is your prayer?

____

____

Psalm 39

Truth — This life cannot compare with eternity.

Issues and points — When we see sinners prevailing, we tend to think this life is more than a breath, but it is not. And then we will be with Him and what glory that will be!
Effect on the Psalmist — He is struggling with the trials and the hurts of this life and needed to be totally yielded to his Lord.

How am I like the Psalmist — How often am I so caught up in this life and its injuries and hurts, that I forget my Redeemer loves me and will take me, for eternity, to be with Him.

My response — Lord, I need to turn my eyes totally upon You for You supply all of my needs here and in eternity.

My prayer:

Lord, when the enemy seems to prevail,
And everything I do is for naught,
Then, when I am no longer able to stand,
You remind me all this is but a breath.
You, Lord, inhabit eternity,
You also made me Your own,
So what little the enemy seems to win,
Is gone, not to be remembered again.

The reader's response:

How are you like/unlike the Psalmist?

What is your response to the Psalm?

____

____

What is your prayer?

____

____

Psalm 49

Truth — God loves us and will bring us to Himself.

Issues and points — No man could redeem his own soul, but, the Psalmist cries out, "He will redeem my soul!"

Effect on the Psalmist — He rejoices because he knows his God will receive him into eternity.

How am I like the Psalmist — Because of His grace and my resulting trust in Him, I too, am able to rejoice.

My response — Lord, I praise You for saving me for eternity to be with You.

My prayer:

What comfort there is for the believer,
To know when life's ending, it is really beginning,
For as our eternal God has promised
We will live with Him forever.
How long could an unbeliever joy?
What happiness could he have?

After this life, there is no hope,
Just eternity away from the God he spurned.
Lord, cause me to share Your love,
That unbelievers may come to trust in You.
The reader's response:

How are you like/unlike the Psalmist?

____

What is your response to the Psalm?

____

____

What is your prayer?

____

____

Psalm 87

Truth — All of God's children will be with Him some day.

Issues and points — The Psalmist begins by rejoicing at what the Lord did for the children of Israel, but includes believers from all other countries.

Effect on the Psalmist — He, too, rejoices in the Lord's great love for all of His own.

How am I unlike the Psalmist — I selfishly don't think or pray enough for all believers.

My response — Forgive me for being so introverted in thinking only of my own family and own church.

My prayer:

Lord, what a wonderful day that will be,
When Your family gathers from every country.
When Your mercy and grace are so great,
That all who will, have come to You.
You are not the God of one people,
But of everyone who believes in You.

The reader's response:

How are you like/unlike the Psalmist?

____

What is your response to the Psalm?

____

____

What is your prayer?

____

____

Psalm 88

Truth — Wherever God has placed us is where we should be.

Issues and points — God is in total control, operating in love and grace. When we are close to death, the question becomes, do we continue to witness for Him or does He call us home?

Effect on the Psalmist — He "just wanted God to know" (even though he knew his Lord already knew) that if called home, he could no longer tell others about his Lord.

How am I like/unlike the Psalmist — I, too, know that being with the Lord in heaven means I can't tell others here on earth any more about Him. The question, then, is, "Am I spending my time here witnessing for Him?" If not, why does He keep me here?

My response — Lord, cause me to understand that You want me to love You, but also serve You by sharing Your love with others.

My prayer:

You, Lord, are my God and Savior,
And whatever You do is right.
But I wanted to offer my own poor advice,
If I'm with You there, I'm not witnessing here.
Certainly being with You is joy,
And heaven is a most wonderful place,
And though I long to see Your face,
If I'm with You there, I'm not witnessing here.
Take me home or leave me here, that is Your right,
But if I'm with You there, I'm not witnessing here.

The reader's response:

How are you like/unlike the Psalmist?

____

What is your response to the Psalm?

____

____

What is your prayer?

____

____

References

Holy Bible – King James Version. Nashville: Thomas Nelson, Publishers, 1975.

Holy Bible — The New King James Version. Nashville: Thomas Nelson, 1983.

Holy Bible — New International Version, Grand Rapids: Zondervan, 1996.

Keil — Delitsche. Commentary on the Old Testament: Volume V The Psalms. Grand Rapids: Eerdmans, 1973.

Lange, John Peter. Commentary on the Holy Scriptures. Ed. By Phillip Schaff. Grand Rapids: Zondervan.

Parry Arthur. *The Psalms for Today*. Unpublished Manuscript.

Parry, Arthur. *Finding God in the Psalms*. Baltimore: PublishAmerica, 2002.

Psalms — Spurgeon. Edited by McGrath and Packer. Wheaton, Crossways Books, 1993.

Numerical Index of the Psalms